P9-CRD-596

Black Eagle

Black Eagle
General Daniel 'Chappie' James, Jr.

James R. McGovern

The University of Alabama Press

Library of Congress Cataloging in Publication Data
McGovern, James R.
Black Eagle, General Daniel "Chappie" James, Jr.
Bibliography: p.
Includes index.
1. James, Daniel, 1920–1978.   2. Generals—United
States—Biography.   3. United States.   Air Force—Biog-
raphy.   I. Title.
UG626.2.J36M34   1985   355'.0092'4 [B]   84-8
ISBN 0-8173-0179-8

FOR JOAN

Contents

Introduction 3

Chapter 1
Someone Special 7

Chapter 2
Tuskegee Years 25

Chapter 3
Serving with the
Segregated Air Force 41

Chapter 4
Korea 56

Chapter 5
As a Leader 69

Chapter 6
Vietnam 83

Chapter 7
A Returning Warrior 100

Chapter 8
Colonel James and
Colonel Khadafy 109

Chapter 9
Into the Stars 123

Chapter 10
The Last Command 144

Chapter 11
Conclusion 159

Notes 169

Bibliography 187

Index 195

Black Eagle

Introduction

There was little reason for young American blacks to be hopeful if they were raised in the Deep South in the early decades of this century. Youth's typical dreams for fame and fortune were impermissible luxuries for them. Even if one wished to be one's own person, opportunities to be effectively free to choose and to achieve one's purposes were severely limited by enveloping handicaps of education, caste, and political deprivation. Indeed, it was even unlikely that a young black man could be confident for his personal safety if he objected to the discriminatory codes that victimized him. Richard Wright and Charles S. Johnson describe, for example, how the threat of lynching was likely to be in the minds of young blacks growing up at this time.[1] Normally such fears might be overcome by efforts to become so good or so skillful that one's oppressors would acknowledge usefulness and would relent. But capable and accomplished blacks also had much to fear. It was black physicians and other professionals, not sharecroppers, who were targets of crowd abuse during the Atlanta riots of 1906; and Nate Shaw was sent to jail for twelve years in the 1930s probably because he was a competent farmer of independent persuasion.[2] Conditions for blacks in the South were often worse because of their success, thus constituting yet another warning for them to stay in their places and dispelling hope.

Under these conditions despair would have been more realistic for blacks than confidence about the future; extraordinary qualities of personality were required for those blacks who wished to accomplish great things, even more so for those who eventually would do so. The life of General Daniel "Chappie" James, Jr. (1920–1978) is a remarkable American success story because he overcame discouragements of time and place as the youngest of seventeen children of limited-income black parents in the southern city of Pensacola, Florida, to become in 1975 the holder of the highest rank in the history of the peacetime American military—a four-star general.[3] A narration of James's life inevitably focuses both on his unusual confidence and drive, largely products of the teaching and example of his parents, and on the eventual willingness of a changing American system to reward him despite its history of racial discrimination.

In view of his accomplishments, it is understandable that General James's life and career are viewed with pride by many black Americans. In fact, one of his close friends, a mayor in a southern city, speaking for black moderates, related, "After [Martin Luther] King he was the best hero we had." But for all his genuine appeal for some blacks, Chappie also was attractive to many whites with whom he served and associated and from whom he received his military promotions. He appealed to them mainly because he subscribed to traditional American values and because he had the ability to project an attractive, professionally competent image that minimized racial prejudice against him.

James's patriotism was especially refreshing to Americans beleaguered by critics from the 1960s and 1970s, particularly on the issues of Vietnam and Watergate. After his appointment to the public affairs staff in the Department of Defense in 1970 (an appointment that extended to 1974) he became the chief spokesman in the Pentagon to youth and college groups and civic organizations. As a speaker, Chappie invariably began from the premise that the United States, with its faults, was the best country in the world. And as a successful man and beneficiary of the system, in which the status of blacks in his lifetime had changed dramatically, he confidently predicted the best was yet to come. It is not an exaggeration to state that Chappie James, during the troubled 1970–1974 period, was one of the more effective persons working to reconcile divergent groups that threatened to pull the country apart. Throughout his career, however, James participated in vital American political and social experiences, from the days when as a Tuskegee Airman he became one of the first blacks to win wings in the military, to the civil rights demonstration he helped initiate on behalf of integrated facilities for black officers during World War II, his success as a fighter pilot and leader in Korea and Vietnam, and his later association with presidents, cabinet members, and top civilian administrators and newsmen in Washington.

James's importance transcended, however, his unprecedented achievements as a black in the military and his role as a spokesman for American community. Even before the Reverend Jesse Jackson began to emphasize the same goals, James was one of the most important exponents of social improvements for blacks through education and training and the pursuit of personal excellence. His views were, in fact, a kind of amalgam of those of historical adversaries Booker T. Washington and W. E. B. Du Bois—James emphasizing both work and achievement but also the immediate realization of all civil rights for blacks. It was the Tuskegee educator's influence, however (James was graduated from Tuskegee), together with James's mother's individualistic self-help philosophy for blacks, that would prompt him to reject quota systems and automatic entitlements based on race.

The most interesting aspect of a study of Chappie James is surely his personality in the face of his society's and his region's racism: his persistent individualism and drive for personal success as a type of black Horatio Alger figure and his confidence that his society finally would acknowledge abilities of "good Americans" regardless of race or color.

This biography is concerned with why and how he developed that confidence as well as why and how he accomplished what he did.

Literary sources for a study of General James's life largely are located in military records housed at the Albert F. Simpson Historical Research Center, Maxwell Air Force Base, Montgomery, Alabama, and in numerous scrapbooks and tapes of General James's speeches located at his alma mater, Tuskegee Institute, Tuskegee, Alabama. This material was augmented greatly by extensive correspondence and more than one hundred interviews with his family members, blacks and whites who served with him in the air force or government work, and those who came to know him as a friend or social acquaintance in his numerous tours of duty throughout the country and overseas.

The author wishes to acknowledge many persons who contributed to this biography, especially members of the James family; former Pentagon officials Melvin Laird, Jerry Freidheim, and Dan Henkin; Daniel T. Williams, director of archives, Tuskegee Institute; Dr. Arthur Doerr, vice-president, University of West Florida, and Dr. Lucius Ellsworth, dean of the College of Arts and Sciences, University of West Florida, for their moral and financial support during research; and the reference staff in the library at the University of West Florida, especially Bo Gilliam, Dr. Lois Gilmer, and Robert Perdue. Dr. Lois Gilmer also indexed this study. Lastly, many thanks to my wife, Joan, who provided steady encouragement.

1. Someone Special

Chappie James was born in 1920 in Pensacola, Florida, a historic gulf coast port city with a relatively cosmopolitan population. The crowd on Palafox Street, the city's main thoroughfare, usually included a rich mixture of townsfolk black and white, American sailors and marines, hulking longshoremen, seamen from several countries, and recent Italian and Greek immigrants. This heterogeneity encouraged Booker T. Washington, who had visited Pensacola in 1900, to describe the city as a "healthy community so necessary to our people."[1] At that time local blacks had invited white friends to attend Washington's talk at the Opera House, and they did so in impressive numbers.[2] In truth, there were good reasons for Washington's optimistic appraisal, and it was shared by many local blacks, especially those who had prospered.

In the early years of the new century, black businessmen had desirable locations on Palafox Street. In addition, substantial black businesses including grocery and furniture stores were located only a block from Palafox.[3] The good-looking homes of black professional and business classes were still other signs of a substantial black bourgeoisie as were the existence of at least two private schools.[4] Pensacola's growing black population (9,182), surpassing that of whites in 1900, naturally supplied a broad economic base to support a number of professional men and women, including several physicians, many esteemed ministers, approximately twenty teachers, and the editor of a good newspaper, the *Florida Sentinel*. Blacks also operated numerous small businesses and entered skilled jobs that mainly served the black community. One of Pensacola's sixteen builders in 1903 was black, as were five dressmakers out of the city's twenty-five, three owners of meat markets of twenty-five, ten restaurants (two on South Palafox) of twenty-six, thirteen of one hundred groceries, three of twenty-six saloons, and one undertaker.[5]

Although the races remained socially distinct in Pensacola, many blacks nevertheless lived on the same streets as whites. A total of 991 blacks lived biracially on streets with 848 whites in the city in 1905, nearly 10 percent of the city's population residing on integrated blocks.[6] While there were three major areas of black population concentration in 1905, none could yet be described as a ghetto.

Living beside whites and working for them as servants and later with them as public employees or independent businessmen had especially important cultural consequences for a black elite. They internalized the good style and gentility of the families for whom they worked. Older blacks declare that they had excellent personal relationships with their employers if the latter regarded them as trustworthy.[7] Those fortunate enough to be on good terms with influential whites remained hopeful for the future even when race conditions for blacks worsened.[8]

A number of factors converged to reduce opportunities for most blacks between 1900 and 1920, the year of Chappie James's birth. A temporary majority of blacks in the city's population may have triggered the reaction;[9] the desire of the city's commercial interests for rapid progress unencumbered by its large uneducated black population was also a factor, and the fear of whites that Pensacola was becoming overrun by black "riffraff" from Alabama and Mississippi, who were unlike Pensacola's black population and to whom the whites objected, also contributed.[10] Furthermore, in-migration that accompanied the boom of the early 1900s brought not only blacks who were objectionable but also whites from farming areas in Alabama who objected to them.[11] Lastly, the city's economic slump in the 1910s embittered relationships between laborers of both races who were forced to compete for fewer jobs. Antiblack feeling therefore accompanied economic decline and provided a convenient rationale to justify job expropriation of blacks by whites. As a result, while the size of the black population remained relatively unchanged in the 1910s, the white population nearly doubled.[12] A Jim Crow ordinance on streetcars was passed by the city council and, after a veto by the mayor on grounds of constitutionality, was passed again and put into effect in October 1905.[13] The local Democratic party instituted an all-white primary election the same year. Blacks also were segregated at public amusements, restaurants, railroad stations, and in cells in the city jail.[14]

The same desire to suppress blacks was expressed in other forms. Whites began to move out of racially mixed neighborhoods and blacks slowly became locked into specific residential areas. Pensacolians living on biracial streets became less numerous.[15] Meanwhile, the editor of the *Pensacola Journal* called for racial segregation in housing because "numerous blocks all over the city are depreciated in value because of the fact that some negro residents are there."[16] He called for a strict color line "to eliminate friction between the races." In the same year (1911), Englewood Heights, a choice subdivision on the west side of the city, opened with restrictions "against nuisances and negroes."[17] Earlier, a laundry that followed "sanitary procedures" had announced it "took work from white people only."[18] Creoles also lost their identity as separate persons in the city directory and came to be listed as colored, suggesting that the slightest racial impurity warranted social stigma.[19]

Racist feelings assumed their most virulent form in the lynchings of blacks, the city's first recorded lynchings "in a long period of years."[20]

The full imposition of Jim Crow laws did not fall with equal severity on all blacks in Pensacola. The older black families, who had worked for white families as domestics or had become public servants as teachers, mailmen, or barbers who performed work essential to the white community, still benefited from close contacts with whites. Their social and economic advantages, especially their opportunities to associate on friendly terms with prominent whites, even encouraged them to aspire to a goal of equality with whites despite segregationist pressures.[21]

Chappie James was raised in this type of black family. His resolve to overcome discrimination and to excel were directly attributable to the strong personalities of his parents and to the effective understanding and teaching of the success ethic by his mother. Daniel James, Sr. (Poppa to his family), was a tall, dark-skinned, good-looking man who had moved to Pensacola from rural Alabama. He illustrated strong and enterprising characteristics once he arrived in the port city despite the fact that he was a black migrant laborer with only minimal formal schooling. He was employed first as a lamplighter for the city of Pensacola and later in the municipal gas plant where coke was converted under high temperature into gas. His latter occupation required skill— to regulate valves to obtain optimal conditions for producing gas—as well as labor, and he supervised others while he worked beside them, ten to twelve hours per day, six days a week. Few blacks, if any, had more responsible jobs with the city. He illustrated the same kind of initiative in courting and marrying Lillie A. Brown, a light-skinned, attractive woman at a time when differences in color largely negated the marital prospects of dark-skinned black men with lighter black women. He also chose to live in a desirable neighborhood for blacks and avoided the area around Railroad Avenue where many poor black migrants lived. Similarly, he scorned as second class those ignorant migrants from Alabama who came up to his porch and strummed on their guitars. Gainful employment was the key to his sense of self-esteem and he used every opportunity to demonstrate its importance to his children. One of the children, for example, was appointed each Saturday to bring Poppa's warm noon meal to the gas plant. Neighbors could set their watches by the punctuality of the performance. If father were inconvenienced by as much as a minute on the job, the child would be chastised verbally and perhaps spanked that night. Daniel James also expected job performance from his boys, especially in gardening, cutting wood, and taking care of the animals; "Lil, did you get hold of those boys?" he would ask his wife. And if someone in the neighborhood reported that one of his boys was "carrying on," that boy was assured an uncomfortable seat at home that night. All the children of Daniel and Lillie James were impressed by their father's ambition and his exemplary devotion to the work ethic.[22]

Poppa James, for all his hard work and sustenance, represented the old ways of American blacks. At best he was merely an aristocrat among manual laborers. He had few prerogatives—a drink in the late afternoon and an occasional opportunity to indulge a young child or grandchild. He foresaw neither better times and opportunities for his children nor the role of education as a vehicle for the progress of blacks. In fact, he wanted his sons to be farmers. If Poppa tried to find success as a black in traditional, restricted ways, his wife, Lillie James, represented new possibilities for blacks. Though, as a mother of a very large family, her opportunities for personal freedom were severely restricted, she embodied the aspirations of successful, modern blacks for education and personal refinement.

Mrs. Lillie A. James belonged to the black elite in Pensacola and shared its perceptions and sense of opportunity. Her mother had served as a domestic for one of Pensacola's wealthy families. Her father was a mailman, one of the very few blacks selected for such a position of public trust. Her family lived in an area of attractive houses inhabited by light-skinned colored persons, and she was the beneficiary of a high school equivalent education in Catholic schools at St. Joseph's, the neighborhood parish for the elite black community. This social background explains her unusual interest in quality education for blacks in Pensacola after her marriage to Daniel James, Sr., in 1893.[23] Lillie James knew from experience that blacks could make progress socially if they were educated and if they desired to improve themselves; but she feared that public schools for black children would only handicap them by inferior discipline and low student expectations.[24]

A heavy woman of medium height, Mrs. James's appearance was distinguished by an intelligent face and penetrating eyes. Her manner was decisive and her personality was marked by unusual energy and charisma. She was happy in her home with her dominant husband, especially inasmuch as he gave her free reign in the raising of the children (except, of course, in their work responsibilities about the house or in helping him) and even more so as he got older and mellowed (Dan Jr. was never spanked by his father).[25] Mrs. James loved to cook and spent hours over her big wooden clay-top stove preparing delicacies with sumptuous results: catfish broiled with onions and seasoned with lemon; beans that were allowed to boil all day and to which she added sautéed onions, garlic, syrup, and long strips of bacon; baked and stuffed red snapper; rare gumbos with special homemade spices and sauces; and homemade bread. A sack of oysters was regularly in view on the James's back porch on Saturday night, to be opened and dropped in a jar by lamplight late that night because Sunday morning meant a special treat: oysters with Lillie James's rolls made the night before. She also saw that there were special foods around the house for her children and their friends: bunches of bananas, crates of grapes, and molasses to make "Syrup Billy," a sweet, long bread sandwich.

She was nurturant in her feelings for children as well. They recall that she sat up all night with them when they were ill, and if they hurt anywhere she kissed them to make them well. She shared in their problems and exercised patience and restraint when they first made mistakes. But Lillie James's tolerance for their shortcomings had decided limits.

She felt compelled to attain perfectionistic goals and she transmitted that same drive to her children, at times with unreasonable, even obsessive commitment. In effect she demanded that her children, as well as those she would teach in her private school, exert themselves to their very limits of ability and endurance.[26] Lillie A. James would realize her most cherished goals for blacks by establishing a private school in her backyard for black children in grades one to eight. There, through that medium, she could combine her insistent prompting for perfection in those around her and her belief that whites would acknowledge excellence in blacks if they performed well.

Every child attending "Miz Lillie's" school heard the headmistress say over and over: "Never let anyone your size beat you doing anything"; and each one learned the "Eleventh Commandment," "Thou shalt never quit." It was repeated so often in the classroom that it came to take precedence over even the original Ten Commandments.[27] Every feature of the Lillie A. James School, the teaching and the training, was geared to the students' future success. The students' lively musical greeting to the teacher and her reply ("the same to you") taught the importance of being pleasant to those in authority and the expectation that they would reciprocate if approached correctly. Singing the math tables, the method used to help students remember, not only was fun but assured skills on par with whites. The pledge to the flag and a patriotic song declared the importance and necessity of working within the system; singing the alphabet both forward and backward by young scholars provided a sense of mastery and conveyed an obvious message that more was expected of them than ordinary students. Nor was spelling left to chance. Flash cards were used, but basically students learned competitively through spelldowns with the class divided and lined up on both sides of the classroom and with the teacher's sympathy and peer pressure all on the side of the survivors. Because Miz Lillie's school placed critical emphasis on speech, especially avoiding southern speech idiosyncrasies, students gained confidence in speaking with cultivated whites. Annual plays before large public audiences were a feature of the school year designed for the same effect.

Mrs. James was equally determined to teach her students proper social conduct for self-respect and to win the respect of whites. "If they say you are dirty," she advised her children, "make sure you are clean; if they say you are afraid, make sure you are brave; if they say you are dishonest, make sure you take nothing that is not yours."[28] The practice of each student's placing five cents, the daily tuition, in a cigar box on the teacher's desk underscored adherence to another American folkway—self-help.[29] Blacks were not, she taught, justified in feeling sorry for themselves or being angry toward whites. Such people were miserable and dragged others down with them. When she spanked her own daughter for drinking from a water fountain for whites, it was because Mrs. James believed that blacks should be law abiding despite the inequity of segregated facilities.[30] With the aid of fair-minded whites they would finally strike down adverse laws, but blacks first would have to work within the system. By demonstrating excellence, giving example, and finally developing alliances with sympathetic whites, they would best help themselves to become first-class citizens.

Given her fierce and unrelenting plans for promoting excellence among blacks, Miz Lillie had little tolerance for those who refused to improve themselves. There was no acceptable excuse for a student who repeatedly was shown how to do things and failed, or who wasted time, perhaps falling asleep at the desk or going into the bathroom without permission. Lillie James would have taken comfort from B. F. Skinner's theories on contingencies of reinforcement had she been living in the 1960s, because she actively was employing them fifty years earlier. She was warm and complimentary toward those who improved or did well, patient with first offenders, but positively merciless with those who were repeatedly unproductive. She used the rod against unregenerate boys or girls in the presence of their classmates. And at times her insistence on students' achievements could lead to frightening, perhaps traumatic experiences for her charges. She collared repeated offenders and pushed their heads over the aperture of a shallow well in the school's backyard, reminding them that their future safety was conditional on their future application. Her ultimate reprisal was to seal a young incorrigible in a potato sack. She would then light a paper close to the sack and fan smoke in the direction of the terrified occupant.[31]

Blacks in Pensacola admired Lillie James and respected her school despite some of her unusual methods because they, too, yearned for a better future for their children and they recognized the value of her exemplary guidance. Parents condoned her severe disciplinary practices as being in the children's best interests and sometimes even encouraged her to chastise their children at school for infractions committed while the children were home. Even when the younger children fled to their homes to avoid her pedagogical demands or punishments, parents brought them back with "All right, Miz Lillie, he is all yours right now." A woman domestic had to sacrifice to pay twenty-five cents a week for the education of her child when her weekly wage was only four dollars, but it was worth it to know that the child would be directed properly. For parents with greater incomes, Miz Lillie's education provided the foundation that would lead to good high school standing and admission to Florida A & M, Tuskegee, or maybe even Fisk. These mothers and fathers cited with pride the names of the community's doctors, lawyers, and teachers who once sat in Miz Lillie's chairs, resembling their own sons and daughters.[32] As her own son, Dan Jr., would later reminisce, "There are a lot of walking monuments to my mother's love, faith and skill. I would not try to count the number who found a sense of purpose and direction and set of values that sustain them to this day."[33]

Dan and Lillie James and their large family lived in a five-room, "shotgun" style wooden house at 1606 N. Alcaniz Street, where Mrs. James bore her seventeen children.[34] It looked like hundreds of similar houses in the black neighborhood, and like them it squeaked at night as its pine wood expanded and contracted with temperature changes. The early years of marriage had been difficult with so many children—though disease, poor medical care for blacks, and the decision by some older children to leave Pensacola resulted in no more than nine children being at home at any one time. In a supreme misfortune, two James babies, twins, died of pneumonia while waiting all day in a white doctor's office because whites received attention before blacks. By 1920, the year of Dan Jr.'s birth, economic pressures on his parents had eased considerably. Birth records attest that only seven of the James's children were then alive and only three children were still at home; Charles, born in 1910; Lillie, 1914, named for her mother; and the new baby. The Daniel James family was then slightly better off than their hardworking neighbors. Dan James, Sr., owned additional property in the 1600 block of Alcaniz and paid higher taxes than those around him. His family also owned cows and chickens and pasture land. Foods were plentiful and varied at the James house; the younger children had individual pets and in the 1930s the family would own a radio, which meant its front porch became ringside for the entire neighborhood during the Joe Louis fights.[35]

The James family's inculcation of the work ethic and goal of success in their children had a particularly strong impact on Daniel James, Jr. Despite the presence of other children in the household, he was such a favorite of his mother's attention and teachings that his role closely resembled that of an only child. His mother's insistent capacity for nurture focused on him because at age forty-four she was unlikely to have other children and he was the only boy left under wing—Charles already having made a reputation for himself as an athletic prodigy. To complete the picture, Dan Jr. suffered from a number of childhood sicknesses that required his mother's continuous attention. Until he was seven years

James family in 1919, the year before Daniel James, Jr.'s birth. Back row: *Tony, Frank, Mason, Francis;* front row: *Charles, Lillie, Mrs. James, Mr. James, Willie.*
(Courtesy of Lillie Frazier)

old "Dan Baby," as his mother called him (and a name that caught on among his youthful friends), fell asleep each night while being rocked on her broad lap. Dan Sr. offered no objection to the close tie between mother and son. He allowed his wife and older daughters to raise Dan Jr., who virtually lived in the kitchen while his mother baked and cooked and hung the men's coveralls to dry near the stove.

The emotional interdependency between Lillie A. James and Dan James, Jr., would have a powerful effect on Dan Jr.'s childhood development and later adult life. It is not surprising, in view of his mother's extraordinary personality and the fact that she was also his teacher, that he would try exceptionally hard to please her and even to identify with her. As a youngster in his mother's school he was a good boy and a diligent student who avoided fights, and his favorite after-school game was playing school and acting the part of the teacher, speaking correctly and correcting others' speech.[36] Lillie James's perfectionist expectations affected Dan Jr. throughout his life. He was never shown the deep well or invited into the potato sack—indeed, was seldom spanked—but only because he tried incredibly hard to win his mother's approval. Because she would withhold her love until her son's deeds were done extraordinarily well—because achievements were means rather than ends for her—young Dan probably never quite felt he was doing enough. The effect in Dan Jr. was to bring intellectual and emotional forces together to produce an extraordinary personality. Many persons, friends, and acquaintances, would observe: "Chappie James seemed to be a phenomenon—a larger than life person." He often is described by others as a "dynamo," a bundle of energy "always on the go," or "extraordinary."[37] He had from his mother's teachings and example a sure sense of direction and rationale, and from her exorbitant demands a fear that he might not measure up. Thus his life became a pursuit of the appropriate strength to silence those fears, a triumph of will. The most remarkable feature of this quest for greatness was that it did not become rigidly compulsive or an obsession dangerous to other persons; rather it was leavened by humor and mirth and fraternity, also products in part of his family background and his mother's own warmth.

When Dan Jr. left his mother's school and entered high school, a young thirteen, he was still fondly called "Dan Baby" by his friends. He became increasingly sensitive to that name and to his being tied so closely to his mother and to her values. His father's strong, dominant personality surely provided sufficient example for this reaction. He was now going to be a man and would behave accordingly—not just any man, of course, but one who would succeed as his mother's teachings dictated, in a special, even spectacular manner.

Men and boys worked hard and played sports; they did not sit around and talk about school. There were to be no more games about school with a female cousin who was now advised she would best sit and watch his baseball games at a safe distance because "we sling our bats."[38] Furthermore, he would be a flier, not an unusual aspiration among young men raised near the naval air station in Pensacola, but unusual for blacks. When he pointed to one of the training planes overhead and declared his intention, everyone, especially the older kids, laughed because they knew flying, like certain park benches and theater entrances, was for whites only; but Dan Jr. remained undaunted.[39] He also enjoyed sitting with his friends in the balcony of the Isis Theater to watch the Pathe News films of the army-navy football games, especially to see the cadets (there was no use watching the midshipmen, because there were no blacks at the naval academy). They went to catch sight of Benjamin O. Davis, Jr., the son of the army's only black general and West Point's only black cadet, before he was lost in a blur of white faces. Dan Jr.'s ambition finally led him to adopt a nickname that spelled masculine prowess. Dan's brother, Charles, had been nicknamed "Chappie." He had gone on to star in football and baseball at Florida A & M and was the first of the James family to graduate from college. He became a teacher and athletic coach. Dan surprised his friends with his insistence that they now call him "Little Chappie," almost as if his new name would make everyone forget "Dan Baby" and give him magical entry into the world of strong men. He also was determined to win praise from his peers for being "a hell of a nigger"—that is, successful with women, a pursuit that typified his behavior for many years to come.[40]

When Dan, or "Little Chappie" as some of his friends called him, left his mother's school in 1933 and entered Washington High School, his new principal, Vernon McDaniel, provided him with an attractive role model. McDaniel, a dedicated educator who believed that schools for blacks must be on par with those for whites, was an illustrious father figure for his students. He not only memorized the phone numbers of all his students so as to be able to call their parents if they were truant but he also drove his car past the honky-tonks and pleasure spots in the black areas during school nights and even on weekends to assure that his students remained home. A medium-sized man, he carried a strap and could bring his problem students to heel quickly. To the alarm, "Here comes Mr. Mac," unsuspecting students, posing as adults on the town, could be seen running for safety in all directions.

Vernon McDaniel labored in the 1930s with a dilapidated wooden school building, located on a sand dune that faced an unpaved street, but Washington High had quality inside. McDaniel had declared his goals to the white school superintendent three days after his appointment and arrival in Pensacola: "How can you teach chemistry without chemicals, biology without microscopes, and physics without a beam balance?" He got what he wanted and with the aid of a faculty, all of whom had college degrees, developed good programs in science and math, including advanced algebra and trigonometry, Latin and French. Strict standards were applied in all disciplines, and the graduates performed well when they went away to college. "Mr. Mac" made a strong impression on Dan James, who invariably impersonated him at the annual student entertainment night. Dan's mimicking of the principal in clothes, manner, and speech was so expert that the audience was convulsed. It was a compliment, of course, to "Mr. Mac," because the young man never bothered to master the idiosyncrasies of any of his other professors; and it was another sign of Dan's turn to masculine identifications.

Dan James was barely seventeen when he graduated from high school, while many of his classmates in these depression years (1933–1937) were eighteen and nineteen. He was a middling student who preferred "well-roundedness" to proficiency in academics (or as McDaniel observed, "if there were a marble shooting contest, he wanted to be in it"). His ambition, typical of his personality needs, was to be seen and to be well liked. He sang in the chorus and glee club, and he played football, but with modest results. Washington High had outstanding teams in the mid-1930s and went undefeated in two successive seasons, one of its players having a remarkable string of successful field goals and points after touchdown, which he booted with either foot. "Little Chappie," as Dan liked to be called on the gridiron, couldn't compete in this company. But because being second-best was intolerable for him, he began to illustrate in high school football what would become a lifelong response to disappointment. He ignored it and conducted himself as if he were, nevertheless, the number one man on the team. In the words of his coach, "He was enthusiastic and felt he was steadily improving, and he was a great source of inspiration to the other players. He would volunteer to go to the other end of the field to pick up the football and he didn't mind carrying the water bucket if no one else was around to do it. He was always cheerful and never sulked. Somehow, he left you with the impression that he was going to get somewhere, even in football."[41]

That same insistence on superior standing and recognition characterized other associations with his older classmates. They accepted Dan's needs to excel without taking offense because his approach, even when he was boasting, was pleasant. Occasionally, when his ambition lost all proportion and he talked up his accomplishments, or told a bigger story about himself than anyone else could imagine possible, or invented his own history as a way of topping a classmate's humble recounting from a textbook, someone in the group familiar with his routines would say, "Shut up, Dan," and that would silence him temporarily. One of his classmates observed, "Chappie said, 'I am the greatest' so many times he convinced himself and half-convinced others." What was remarkable about his high school years, the first period of his life in which he was forced to be openly competitive, was his ability to deal with personal inadequacies in a way that did not impair his confidence. He had enough ego to remain positive, to practice to improve his skills, and ultimately, if necessary, to deny seeming contradictions.

There was one major exception to this response—Dan Jr.'s setback when he attempted to win a prize at the local Major Bowes Amateur Hour competition for blacks. Winners would compete at regional levels and eventually on the Major Bowes program on national radio. Because the local shows usually drew many pretentious people, judges ruled that a contestant could be forced to step down if the performance was considered poor or mediocre. Dan Jr., who had an attractive voice, had just begun the singing of "Alone" when the dreadful gong of the judges' displeasure sounded. It was mortifying; he had been judged incompetent. But what disturbed him most was that the verdict had been delivered with a finality that left no room for contradiction. Nor could he work to improve the outcome. Amazingly, years later, indicative of his tireless pursuit for superiority, Chappie James still bore hurt and embarrassment over this incident of his youth in which he had failed irrevocably.[42]

In the spring of 1937 James's father died just as Dan Jr. was about to graduate from high school and enroll in college. At that time Dan Jr. was working at a downtown recreation center and attempting to save money for his college education. When he returned home from work on an April afternoon and learned that his father had died of a heart attack that day, he became very quiet and remained so for several days— there was no weeping, just quiet. As the shock of the event gradually passed, Dan Jr. had some very uncomfortable feelings that he might not be able to attend college. He feared that he would, instead, wind up doing lackey jobs and hanging around street corners, pool halls, and the bars; but his family rallied behind him. Older brother Tony, employed as a mechanic at the naval air station, advised him to carry through his plans, and he and sister Lil, employed as a high school teacher near Pensacola, provided monetary assistance while Dan Jr. helped himself with a variety of jobs after school. With financial support, he resolved to matriculate at the best-known college for blacks in the Deep South, Tuskegee Institute, where the faculty included the renowned Dr. George Washington Carver.[43]

*Mrs. Lillie A. James. This photograph was taken in the 1950s when
Mrs. James was in her seventies. She was still actively teaching in her
school at this time.*
(Courtesy of Lillie Frazier)

As he left for Tuskegee in September 1937, "Little Chappie," the name he would prefer to plain "Dan" in the more competitive environment there, was primed for success. He had a positive attitude toward life and abundant energy to experiment in a variety of undertakings. He also had a consummate need to prove himself and to establish his importance, a need that could lead to braggadocio but that was mostly good-natured and consequently inoffensive for someone so ambitious. His main advantage at this time in his life was, however, his confident direction, his sense of how to succeed. This was, of course, the principal legacy of the rich educational experiences of his childhood provided by both his father and his mother.

2. Tuskegee Years

Tuskegee Institute, founded by Booker T. Washington in 1881 in the gently sloping countryside of Macon County in the Alabama Black Belt, was the ideal college for the maturation of Chappie James's legacy from Pensacola. The college's philosophy on race relations reinforced what he had learned at home. It also offered numerous opportunities to James, now physically robust and tall (6'4"), to win acclaim as an athlete and campus leader. Finally, when World War II broke out, Tuskegee Institute would sponsor a flight training program, leading to a commission for James in the Army Air Corps and fulfillment of his boyhood dream, a career as a military pilot.

Booker T. Washington's influence still pervaded education and campus life at Tuskegee in 1937, twenty-two years after his death. Students read his works, spoke with teachers who remembered him, and noted the impressive statue resembling a campus centerpiece that portrayed the noted educator liberating a humble black from the slavery of ignorance. Washington would substitute for that ignorance industrial education and the "work ethic" to equip blacks with skills, income, and attitudes that would make them indispensable to the biracial economy in the South. He believed this process eventually would guarantee political justice for blacks because political power "would come to those with prosperity and intelligence regardless of race, color or geographic location." There were, of course, flaws in his reasoning. Tuskegee's founder overstated the opportunities for and the effects of biracial joint-interest economics, while he underestimated the emotional and psychological factors that perpetuated racial discrimination. Whites in the South would commit acts of violence against blacks and impose Jim Crow restrictions against them precisely as they became more prosperous or if they gave evidence of self-reliance. Washington had to confront a severe contravention of his idea on race even as it applied to his own family when he learned in 1911 that whites had sued the Pullman Company for allowing Mrs. Washington to ride in a Pullman car with whites to Memphis. Surely, Washington was optimistic when he assumed that success in the United States for blacks, as well as whites, was merely a matter of being worthy and trying to achieve.[1]

Despite their temporary setbacks, Washington directed blacks, especially those who attended Tuskegee, to "cast down your buckets" in the South and to develop habits, skills, and morality that would win respect among southern whites. He provided direction, if not an infallible credo. He never called for permanent second-class status for blacks but, rather, asserted that quality was the guarantor of their complete participation. Meanwhile, blacks who responded positively to his admonitions for self-responsibility, hard work, personal refinement, and adaptation to the society were stronger for doing so. He provided, as he did for Chappie James, a rationale and goal direction for black achievers that reinforced their own drives for excellence.

Although the students at Tuskegee in the 1930s came from a variety of economic backgrounds, most were poor and regarded their opportunity to attend as a great privilege. They were also proud of Tuskegee's history and the founder's achievements in providing them with an opportunity to improve themselves. Students felt a special responsibility to excel at Tuskegee on these accounts despite old-fashioned social and disciplinary codes that already seemed passé to many of them in the 1930s. Fighting on campus, for example, was a basis for expulsion and so was a boy's putting an arm around a girl; and boys' visits to the girls' dorms were forbidden (girls' visits to boys' dorms were unthinkable as well as prohibited). Transgressions meant consignment to "Chehaw," the tiniest of railroad stations near Tuskegee from which offenders were ignominiously dispatched home. Students were so glad for the opportunity to attend Tuskegee, however, that they generally swung into the routines, including proper dress, strict punctuality for class, and sexual abstention, without complaint.[2]

Dan Jr. went to Tuskegee without a clear idea about his career goals, finally settling on physical education, but he was not motivated to study, as his typical B and C grades indicated. His main interests at Tuskegee were joining the athletic teams and becoming a recognized campus leader. He relished being called "Chappie," and his classmates readily obliged because it had become ridiculous for them to call a man of his commanding stature "Little Chappie." He also enjoyed "Big Lumbering Dan," with its homage to his size and power.[3]

Chappie's leadership was assured once he made the forty-man football squad as a freshman. That first year he was a trifle timid scrimmaging against the varsity, but his teammates recall he was an invariable source of inspiration for other players. When his close friend, freshman quarterback Robert "Red" (short for red-hot) Moore, was discouraged after being roughed up by the varsity, Chappie declared, "You can be the greatest football player in the world, Red, if you want to be."[4] Chappie enjoyed being with the athletes, and even as a freshman he made all the football trips on the school's antique bus, the Blue Goose, including the coveted trip to Chicago to play Wilberforce University under the lights in Soldiers Field. Freshman players were obliged to serve baloney sandwiches, the players' food boxed for the trip, and to purchase milk along the way. Tuskegee boxed those sandwiches because they were economical but also to save players the embarrassment of having to stop someplace where they might be refused service. On the ride back to

Tuskegee, even in that freshman year when he did not play, Chappie was a source of fun and fellowship, usually providing songs as entertainment for the other players. Athletes at Tuskegee were an elite group, the leaders in student activities. Many matriculated there because it had a reputation for being the Notre Dame of black football, its coach, Cleve Abbott, another Knute Rockne. Abbott had been an army officer in World War I; the players respected his toughness and discipline and submitted willingly to his grueling scrimmages on hot September afternoons. Years later, Chappie James acknowledged his debt to Coach Abbott: "He taught me how to be a proud man. When the national anthem was being played, we didn't stand around kicking the sod, we stood at attention with our helmets over our hearts."5

Dan James started at tackle for Tuskegee as a sophomore; he was also by that time on the first team of campus leaders. At campus socials at two o'clock on Sunday afternoons, other students acknowledged his presence with a "Hey Chap" or a playful "Hello Big Man." He usually had a crowd of special friends around him in one corner of the activities room from which would come a lot of joshing and laughter. James carried himself in his campus activities, however, as if he were destined for greatness. One friend recalls, "When he entered the cafeteria door, many heads would turn his way, because he looked like an 'ambassador' even though his fellow students knew he was just coming to get his grits like everyone else." Another contemporary acknowledges, "We knew he had something different and we all wished that we had it."6

Chappie's positive spirit also had caught the attention of Coach Abbott, who gave him special responsibilities to supervise the other players at practice and in recruiting high school prospects. Chappie had another special qualification for that job; he was the only member of the team to own a dress suit, a gift from his sister Lil. Many high school players were attracted to Tuskegee on his account; he became their leader once they arrived on campus and he introduced them to the student body. He thereby illustrated a skill that came naturally and one he repeated throughout his later military career, that of doing loyal favors for those younger than he (later, those of lesser rank), thereby developing an indissoluble band of friends who promoted Chappie's as well as one another's interests. One fellow student recalls: "He came right in just like the police force to aid his friends, and if one of them was bothered, he would say to the brotherhood, 'let's go and help him out.' "[7]

Chappie's personality—masculine, yet considerate—and the fact that he was an athlete and singer made him extremely popular with young women on campus. June Townsend, his high school favorite, was at Florida A & M in Tallahassee and he still admired her, especially in the summers when both returned to Pensacola. But Chappie had an eye for young women, and June could not retain his allegiance during the college year.

His serious romance came with Dorothy Watkins, an attractive, tall, light-complected high school senior. She was raised in the community of Tuskegee where her father, a former teacher, had been associated with Tuskegee Institute and later worked in a machine shop in a veterans hospital. The Watkins family lived comfortably in a good-sized, attractive house and owned a car. Dorothy was a shy person raised in a sheltered home dominated by an authoritative father. When she was a senior at Tuskegee High School, then operated by the college and located on its campus, she had not yet gone out on a date. Other high school senior girls had their eyes on the college men, of course, and especially Chappie James. "All the girls were crazy about him," Dorothy related, "but nobody could be that wonderful and so I developed an immediate dislike for Chappie James."[8]

Chappie noticed Dorothy for the first time at the Memorial Day dance in 1938. Because most of the college students had gone home, high school students were permitted to attend. Chappie walked over to Dottie and cavalierly extended his hand without comment. It was customary for high school girls to accept this type of nonchalant gesture as an invitation to dance, especially coming from lordly college freshmen. Dottie looked the other way and Chappie was forced to stand with his hand outstretched ridiculously.

The next time, a dance or two later, he managed a verbal invitation and was shocked when she said no. Dorothy thereby piqued Chappie's fierce need for victories and attention. He came back again and again until she consented to dance. She finally allowed him to walk her to the college gate where her father picked her up after the dance, but she continued to play hard to get, and Chappie increasingly felt a need to overwhelm her. So as they walked out together, he divulged the reasons for his singular importance. He was, he informed her, "*the* Chappie James, *the* Daniel James, Jr., *the* football hero." But Dottie replied, "Oh, you are. Well, I don't think you are so hot, and besides I think you are conceited and stuck up." Chappie was crushed, but, of course, her reaction forced him to try harder, and he soon began to court her devotedly. They would wed November 3, 1943.[9]

James should have been a Tuskegee graduate by the time of his marriage, but he had been expelled from college the previous year, just two months before graduation. He had finally carried his "Big Lumbering Dan" style too far (inasmuch as the college administration already was sensitized by his role in prior episodes). He had responded to insinuations from a fellow student that he was carrying on with a coed by challenging his accuser to a fight. Because Dan beat his opponent in a vicious brawl on campus in an arena provided by his friends locking arms to simulate a ring, the whole matter was too flagrant a violation of college rules to be ignored.

Dismissal might have had devastating consequences for Chappie. He frequently had told his friend Red Moore that "if [I] ever got kicked out of the place [my] mother would die."[10] Circumstances came to his rescue. To fend complaints from the NAACP and the black press over a lack of opportunity for blacks in the Army Air Corps, the Civilian

Aeronautic Administration, at the suggestion of the War Department, had initiated in 1938, with segregationist intent, a
program (the Civilian Pilot Training Program) to train civilian
pilots at several black colleges, including Tuskegee. The War
Department intended to avoid integrated pilot training, even
as it prepared to fulfill the letter of the law, by providing
separate facilities for blacks. Tuskegee was also selected
March 25, 1941, as the exclusive site for training black military as pilots.[11] Black trainees first enrolled in a primary
program, with training given by civilians under contract, and
then moved to an advanced program where all instruction
came from the military.[12]

Chappie James had learned to fly in the CPT Program in his
senior year at Tuskegee, performing exceptionally well. His
instructor, a black, "Chief" Charles A. Anderson, commented, "He had more guts than anyone I had ever seen."
After completing the program James was hired as a civilian
pilot, his source of employment in Tuskegee after expulsion
from college. He also had applied for admission to the air
corps's advanced flying program at Tuskegee as a military
cadet, but because that program was oversupplied with applicants with only ten admitted every five weeks, Chappie
would not enter the all-black cadet program until January
1943.[13]

The "Tuskegee Experiment," as the Army Air Corps
frankly described its cadet program, was designed to test
whether blacks actually could meet the requirements of flying for the military. Care was taken to select top applicants to
ensure that "the experiment" would be fair. Blacks accepted
as cadets met the same standards as whites—intelligence
and reaction tests were administered and a minimum of two
years in college was required. The selection of Tuskegee Institute as the site to test whether blacks could become air
corps pilots also was designed to produce a favorable outcome: the institute was the best-known black college in the
country, and its students were reasonably cosmopolitan and
compatible with the cadets with whom they would socialize.

Furthermore, flying was alien to the experience of all but very few blacks when they entered the flight program and segregation provided them with a chance to learn in a cohesive environment without constant, direct competition with whites. The commandant at Tuskegee, Noel F. Parrish, speculates that "the more confident and talented Blacks" would have done well in integrated squadrons, but "some might have reacted as do many Blacks today in large white universities" with a resulting loss of efficiency and a higher incidence of failure.[14] As it was, over 250 cadets failed to complete a program that commissioned only about 1,000 candidates.[15]

Regardless of the egalitarian intent of the "Tuskegee Experiment," it would be a mistake to assume that its black cadets had equal opportunity with whites to win their wings. Tuskegee's cadets confronted the physical and psychological obstacles of being blacks in the South in the 1940s. They experienced discrimination on their own segregated base; the first white commander posted signs ordering that all blacks use separate facilities from whites. Almost all the white instructors were southern; they were volunteers and good soldiers who enjoyed "the experiment" and worked hard to produce good pilots to help win the war, but their background stimulated anxieties among black trainees who were acutely sensitive to slights. Many cadets at one time or another questioned whether they were being treated fairly or would be treated fairly. Some suspected that no matter how good they became they would wash out because they would be judged "uppity." And whenever a cadet failed out of the program, his peers questioned automatically—was it because he was a deficient pilot or a hard charger?[16]

The civilian environment in and about the community of Tuskegee in Macon County, Alabama, intensified sensitivities among cadets. Greatly outnumbered by blacks, whites dominated the area only through strict application of Jim Crow laws. The cadets, especially the large contingents of "uppity" blacks from the North, merely aggravated the whites' problem of maintaining authority. Besides, Macon County whites were convinced that the "experiment" was a boondoggle and that blacks would prove incompetent for flying. When Colonel Noel Parrish, a Kentuckian and commandant from 1942 to 1946, reported to white friends that black cadets at Tuskegee, upon testing, showed faster reaction time than a group of white cadets from New England, his friends took the information in stride; one of them casually remarked, "Those Yankees always were slow."

Inevitably, explosive situations developed in military-civilian relations in Tuskegee. When a black military policeman saw two local policemen arrest a drunken black soldier on the streets of Tuskegee, he drew his gun and demanded that the serviceman be released in his custody. The startled police complied, but they ran for reinforcements from white townsmen and managed to overcome the MP, clubbed and disarmed him, and took him to jail. Because martial law had not been proclaimed, the civilian police were technically within the law on both scores. But frustration among black servicemen over bullying tactics by the police was so great that once blacks on post heard about the incident they decided to fight back. Two truckloads of armed soldiers, MPs, and airmen headed in the direction of Tuskegee. They were intercepted by Colonel Parrish as they discussed strategy while parked on the Tuskegee campus only three miles from the downtown. Colonel Parrish, fearing an impending clash with firearms, asked the blacks to remain there until the facts could be ascertained. After driving into town he discovered that whites had removed guns from basements of stores and were dispensing them to able-bodied males. The issue finally was resolved when the police surrendered the MP to white military officers who pledged military discipline against him.[17]

Chappie James's response to military life as a cadet was positive. Whatever the frustrations (and apparently he overheard racial slurs directed against cadets while a trainee) or the discomforts of the tense situation in Tuskegee, he would not allow immediate problems to deflect him from his career goals.[18] With graduation would come a second lieutenant's bars, a smart dress uniform, equal status with whites of the same rank, a salary of $327 a month for an aviator with a dependent, and he would be flying airplanes, sufficient benefit by itself. As a cadet James still could enjoy his college antics—such as spraying the dorms at Tuskegee with water from a fire hose—but he generally behaved more like a military professional. His friend, Red Moore, who returned to visit him in 1943 after a year's absence, was struck by the transformation, and when an old friend, now a cadet standing in ranks, blurted out, "Hey Chap" while James was reviewing the troop as a cadet officer, James glowered back as if to say, "Dummy, get with it."

Chappie also helped a number of his friends, especially those from the North, to understand the realities of a military training program in the Deep South. To some, he underscored his mother's Eleventh Commandmant, one cadet recalling that he heard her advice so often that he found a new friend in "Miz Lillie."[19]

Good fellowship, of course, carried the cadets through many difficult days. On one occasion, for example, when a busload of cadets was traveling about two hundred miles to a gunnery range in Florida, they became extremely hungry despite the boxed lunch provided. When the bus reached a lonely sandwich shop splattered with Coke and Dr. Pepper signs, they held council. One of their members could pass for white, so they instructed him to go in and order sandwiches by posing as a white and to "make it good." When the woman behind the counter asked about "the soldiers," he replied that they were "good niggers" and "those niggers would sure appreciate a sandwich, ma'am." She concluded they looked all right inasmuch as they were in uniform and he could take the sandwiches out to their bus. When the hero returned, the others jumped him. He didn't have "to make it that good" by calling them "niggers," too.[20]

Many cadets also found strength in Colonel Benjamin O.

Davis, Jr., leader of the Ninety-ninth Pursuit Squadron at Tuskegee before he was ordered to lead black aviators in combat and departed in April 1943.[21] Later he would command a group in the North African and European theaters, four squadrons made up entirely of black aviators trained at Tuskegee. Davis, whom Dan James had admired in news films as a high schooler, had a father, Benjamin O. Davis, who was the nation's only black general. Benjamin Jr. had been the only black to graduate from West Point (in 1936) since the 1890s. When he was a little boy his father had groomed him for that appointment and the harassment that would go with it by demanding that he perform difficult tasks stoically and with iron will. Davis had no roommates at West Point and was given the silent treatment during his first two years there, but he endured with glacial self-discipline. In training, he helped cadets by his example, not with compassion. He was admired and respected for his professionalism by white officers and, although the cadets probably would have preferred more humanity rather than his magnificent example, they instinctively recognized through him that blacks could perform in the military.

Most cadets also were spurred on by their pride as black Americans and their conviction that the black population in the United States would be encouraged by their success; hence they worked very hard. They knew that when they completed the program they would demolish one more myth of racial incompetence. In World War I it had been artillery—whites in the military argued that blacks could not master the requisite mathematics; now it was flying. One Tuskegee Airman has summarized this attitude: "We knew a lot rested on the success of the experiment. Our flying came at a time when it was necessary to add more pride to black Americans. They were encouraged by stories about us in the black press, and so we gave everything our best effort."[22]

The successful cadets began to fly more complicated aircraft and with their achievements came greater confidence both as pilots and as men. Beginning with the old Steerman

Physical training of cadets at Tuskegee Army Air Field in 1943.
(Courtesy of U.S. Air Force)

Cadets preparing to fly at Tuskegee Army Air Field in 1943. AT-6
aircraft are in background. Major James A. Ellison returns the salute
of Mac Ross, of Dayton, Ohio, as he passes the cadets lined up
during review.
(Courtesy of U.S. Air Force)

biwing, an open-cockpit trainer, they moved up to the more
rapid BT-13s, AT-6s, and then to the swift P-40 Warhawks.
They came to recognize from the mishaps and fatalities of

*Cadets study cross-country flight in Basic and Advanced Flying
School at Tuskegee Army Air Field. Lt. Donald B. McPherson, air
corps director of basic training, explains as cadets look on.
(Courtesy of U.S. Air Force)*

their fellow cadets that their lives were uncertain every minute they were aloft, yet they learned to live and fly in defiance
of that fact. They then became daring—buzzing (Chappie
liked to buzz the dorms at Tuskegee), hedgehopping, and
flying under bridges, one of the airmen losing his life attempting the latter north of Montgomery. Flying conferred feelings
of freedom and competency. Those who succeeded and won
their wings were certain to feel entitlement to equality with
whites in rights and opportunities.[23]

After completion of training, thirty-three officers from
Tuskegee were assigned to the Ninety-ninth Pursuit Squadron and ordered in April 1943 to North Africa. Colonel Par-

*First Tuskegee cadets to win their wings at Tuskegee Army Air Field
in 1943. From left to right: George S. Roberts, Capt. B. O. Davis, Jr.,
Charles DeBow, Lt. Robert M. Long (instructor), Mac Ross,
Lemuel R. Custis.*

rish bade them farewell. He underscored their responsibility
to the nation and to its black population. While the country
was not perfect, he asserted, it was improving and he hoped
that the aviators would "fight and die" if need be for the
worthy cause of protecting democratic ideals.[24]

The Ninety-ninth went into action in early June 1943 and
was active in the invasions of Sicily and Italy. It became a
part of the 332nd Group of four black squadrons in July 1944,
and that outfit engaged in strafing and dive-bombing and
provided fighter escort in Italy, France, Germany, and the
Balkans. Although the first evaluations of the 332nd were
unfavorable (the unit did lack experienced leadership, Davis
having had his wings for only one year when he was asked to
lead his squadron in combat), exhaustive studies and review
boards indeed have verified that blacks can fly in combat.[25]
Their squadrons were neither the best nor the worst in the
Mediterranean and European theaters. The 332nd flew

*Recently graduated cadets inspect cockpit of fighter aircraft at
Tuskegee Army Air Field, 1943.
(Courtesy of U.S. Air Force)*

armed reconnaissance missions in Italy, including Anzio,
and escorted and protected bombers that struck oil refineries
(at Polesti), factories, and airfields in Germany, central Europe, and the Balkans. They also strafed airdromes, rail-
roads, highway bridges, power stations, and other targets.
On March 24, 1945, the 332nd won a Distinguished Unit
Citation for flying an escort mission 1,600 miles round-trip to
attack a tank factory in Berlin and attacking and driving off
interceptors that attempted to interfere.[26] The 332nd also
was entitled to some consideration of distinction because its
fliers had come from further back. Colonel Parrish under-
lined this human dimension, which eluded the statistical
evaluations, when he sympathetically observed: "The fact
that they could operate with the background they had, the
conditions they were under, the suspicions as well as the real

First black pilots to be assigned to a fighter squadron, 1942, Tuskegee Air Base. Lt. Col. Benjamin O. Davis, commanding officer of the 99th Fighter Squadron, posed with the first pilots to be assigned to the unit. From left to right: Front row—*Lt. Herbert E. Carter, Lt. Lee Rayford, Lt. George S. Roberts, Col. Davis, Lt. Lemuel R. Custis, Lt. Clarence Jamison, and Lt. Charles B. Hall;* second row—*Lt. Walter I. Lawson, Lt. Spann Watson, Lt. Alan Lane, Lt. Paul G. Mitchell, Lt. Leon Roberts, Lt. John W. Rogers, Lt. Louis R. Purnell, Lt. James Wiley, and Lt. Graham Smith;* third row—*Lt. Willie Ashley, Lt. Charles Dryden, Lt. Erwin Lawrence, Lt. William A. Campbell, Lt. Willie H. Fuller, Lt. Richard Davis, Lt. Sidney Brooks, Lt. Sherman White, and Lt. George R. Bolling.*
(Courtesy of U.S. Air Force)

fears that they would not be given equal opportunity or recognition or treatment, and the question of precisely what they were fighting for, which was bound to arise—considering all these things, I thought they did better than anyone had a right to expect."[27]

3. Serving with the Segregated Air Force

While it is commonly held by Americans that their country's war with Germany and Japan was a fight for democracy and against racism, United States treatment of its own black and oriental minorities during the war contradicted these lofty purposes. This inconsistency applied even to minorities in military service, persons called upon to risk their lives for the preservation of a nation's ideals even as they themselves were victimized by the nation's prejudices over race. This situation produced racial tensions that generated several explosive incidents, including a major event occurring in a unit to which Daniel "Chappie" James, Jr., was assigned. He was commissioned a second lieutenant in July 1943 and went to Selfridge Field near Detroit where he was reassigned to the 477th Bombardment Group to train in medium-range, multi-engine bombers (B-25s). Black officers in the 477th especially resented their segregated facilities and second class status because some of them had just completed many months of dangerous aerial combat in Europe. This resentment would lead them to refuse to obey an order in wartime and would thrust Lieutenant James, who had joined the dissidents, into events of national significance.[1]

Some high government officials and ranking air corps officers were, of course, dedicated to the success of the black pilots and looked upon their achievements as genuine contributions to winning the war. Most, however, had grudgingly accepted them for training in the first place and later looked upon them as "a problem" that interfered with overall military effectiveness. Ranking white officers were generally more apprehensive that black pilots would have a negative effect on the white military, who were carrying the brunt of the war, than hopeful over contributions blacks might make.[2] Persons of this persuasion, including Brigadier General Frank O. D. Hunter, who exercised command over James's outfit, believed that racial segregation was essential.[3]

Separate but equal, in the military as in civilian society, really meant, of course, racially unequal, as any comparison of the quality of officers' clubs, opportunities for promotion, and social freedom of black and white officers proves.[4] This type of segregation and racial discrimination especially rankled James, who had been taught that qualified blacks were entitled to the same prerogatives as whites. He was particularly incensed because the law, despite the discriminatory practice, prohibited exclusion of black officers from officers' clubs for whites. Army Regulations 210-10 stated specifically that officers' clubs, messes, and similar social organizations must be open for full membership to all officers on duty at a post. If a post limited membership in any particular military organization, it was obliged still "to extend the right of temporary membership to all officers on duty at the post."[5] These rules were not observed by base commanders, however, because they feared the effects of biracial socializing. As long as blacks were located on an all-black base, such as Tuskegee, no problems over inequities arose for officers in command, but at Selfridge there were twelve white pilots and sixty blacks.[6]

Other events at Selfridge undoubtedly angered James and other black officers. In 1943 a drunken white commander shot and wounded a black soldier without reasonable provocation. He later was court-martialed and retired from the service, but the incident must have stirred bitter feelings. There were also the instructions to the Women's Army Corps—WAC—(all white) at Selfridge: they were not to walk freely about the base, nor from work in the control tower without MP escorts, and they were not to socialize with blacks. Another troublesome event occurred on January 1, 1944, when three black officers were ordered out of the officers' club for whites. One squadron commander threatened thereafter to court-martial, on grounds of inciting a riot, any black officers in his command who entered an officers' club for whites.[7] General Hunter, an intense man with a consuming mistrust of blacks, thereupon addressed a large assemblage of black personnel on base. He warned that he would not tolerate blacks and whites using the same facilities or even sitting beside one another in the theater. As Chappie James later recalled:

> They had drawn a line down the middle of the theatre, in Selfridge Field, Michigan (where even the theatres in downtown Detroit were not segregated), and said, "The blacks will sit on one side of this line, and the whites on the other." And so when we, with the full cooperation of most of the whites (who were not in authority and did not agree with this sort of enforced segregation), decided to go on what we called "Operation Checkerboard" after the lights went out in the movie, they turned the movie off and made us go back to our segregated seats. This was a very stupid thing to do, but they did it two or three times a night.[8]

Hunter concluded his presentation with a frank warning to blacks that they must learn their place. While he had no objection to their flying and fighting beside whites against a common enemy, General Hunter cautioned them against unrealistic social expectations, predicting that "Negroes can't expect to obtain equality [in the United States] in 200 years." Separate facilities and clubs were essential, he admonished, because "colored officers weren't ready to be accepted as the equal of white officers." In view of the gravity of the problem and the limits to his patience in dealing with it, Hunter warned that anyone who advocated a mixing of the races on military bases under his command would be treated as "an agitator" and dealt with accordingly.[9] General Hunter's speech had no effect perhaps because morale in the 477th already was so low that its officers chose to ignore his threats. The unit had been substandard from the beginning and it had never become efficient. At first there were no trained bomber pilots, then there were sixty pilots and no bombadier-navigators; later few crews were at the same levels of training.[10] Morale was poor because there were hardly any promotions for blacks, who were generally assigned to positions as assistants to whites (James, for example, a first lieutenant, was assistant operations officer in the 618th Squadron of the 477th).[11] As white commanders became preoccupied with the issue of segregation, blacks in the 477th became even more discouraged. This disgruntlement rubbed off on all other issues and sharpened racial tensions, which, of course, further impaired military effectiveness. Lieutenant James recalled that he and his friends went into the officers' club for whites and ordered drinks, thereby forcing the bartender to close down the club. The black officers left and returned when one of their friends among the white officers called and reported the club was open again and serving.[12] The determination of black aviators to desegregate the officers' club proved a new and baffling predicament for white commanders. While most black officers had accepted their second-class status as civilians and even as cadets at Tuskegee, flying had infused them with new confidence, especially after many of them or their friends had served with Colonel Davis in combat. This temperament would inspire in 1945 a nonviolent sit-in to hasten the day of civil rights in the military, fifteen years before students at Greensboro, North Carolina, would first attempt to integrate lunch counters in civilian society.

The situation at Selfridge was so menacing to white commanders, who believed that repression was the key to order, that the 477th was shipped to Freeman Field, Indiana. Here one of the more serious events of racial unrest in World War II occurred when whites attempted to maintain a separate club for "supervisory personnel." To maintain their privacy they designated blacks, including fliers returning from combat in Europe, as "training personnel." Dissident blacks, determined to challenge this fiction, planned their strategy carefully, avoiding violence and allowing themselves to be arrested and confined to barracks without resistance upon entry to the club for whites. Those arrested were charged with mutiny and disobedience of orders.[13]

The immediate concern of those arrested was whether enough fellow officers would join them and risk this mark on their records. They were especially eager for the support of a number of fliers who had just returned from temporary duty in South Carolina, concerned whether members of this group would be misled into signing a directive from the commanding officer at Freeman. (Blacks were to read and declare they "fully understood" the distinctions that legitimized separate facilities for supervisors and trainees, thereby endorsing the commanding officer's policies of racial discrimination.)[14] The rebels phoned to the field to explain the situation to the returning officers, but the results at first were not reassuring, one captain replying, "Who are you, Lieutenant, to be telling me what I should be doing?" Fears were allayed, however, after an effort was made to reach Chappie James, whose support was deemed important. He replied his concurrence with the decision of the dissidents and assured them that he would influence others to do the same. More than 100 black air corps officers, including Lieutenant James, later refused to sign the directive even after they were warned their actions could be construed as willfully disobedient in time of war. James and the others were prepared to risk their careers, even prolonged incarceration, to attack the military's flagrant inequities. The following day, April 13, they were placed under arrest and sent to Godman Field, Kentucky.

It was an anxious as well as exciting time for the Young

Turks; many were perplexed by the thought that their actions would invite courts-martial. Some expressed fear that this episode would hurt the image of blacks and make them look like deserters or traitors. It bothered them that whites would seize on the situation to prove that blacks were unreliable at times of the country's greatest needs. Everyone agreed that they would attempt to counteract these negative views by presenting their case to the black press and favorable white newspaper editors and by telegrams to the NAACP and to the president. A number of men later prominent in American life assumed leadership roles in the barracks room revolt at this point. William T. "Bumps" Coleman, later secretary of transportation in the Gerald R. Ford administration, became the legal adviser for his fellow officers. Coleman made contact with Thurgood Marshall, a young NAACP legal adviser, later Supreme Court justice, who would advise the accused when some later went to trial. Coleman Young, later to become mayor of Detroit, then also under arrest in the barracks, typed out dispatches to a series of newspapers. Young became especially concerned because of the untimely death of President Roosevelt (April 12), which he feared would have adverse consequences for the black officers' cause.[15] He imagined the group might now be kept in prison forever. Daniel James, Jr., after being placed in custody, became a courier between the arrested officers, surrounded by barbed wire and armed Military Police, and the outside world. The only plane available for carrying orders to and from Washington regarding the controversy was a C-46; so James, the only available pilot checked out to fly the plane, was released. Coleman, Young, and others devised a plan with Chappie before he left. While he performed his assignment for the military, he also would carry Coleman Young's dispatches, slipped through the barbed-wire fence, to persons in the media who were thought friendly to the cause. James's gregariousness had led to contacts with prominent blacks in several cities, thus he had access to both the black and white press, which responded with good coverage.

In the interim, military discipline among the black officers virtually disintegrated. When their commanding officer, a white, entered their barracks, black officers refused to salute and proceeded to ignore him; "some of them were playing knife and some were tossing pennies in the air and when he walked through everyone faced away and nobody said a damned word."[16] The impasse—charges of mutiny against the black officers, their determined resistance to orders enforcing segregation, and their contempt for officers who promulgated these orders—required a quick response from the War Department. Considering the gravity of the situation, the end came quickly. General George C. Marshall approved the release of 101 black officers from arrest in quarters and elimination of charges against them. Of the remaining three, charged with shoving a superior officer, one later paid a fine.[17]

The War Department released the officers on grounds that they did not understand the implications of their actions and were not adequately apprised of the regulations at Selfridge concerning the clubs—a dubious rationale, but the results were salutary. Determined opposition from the black officers and public pressure from the NAACP, the press, and favorable congressmen had carried the day. The War Department soon thereafter chose to review and restate with clarity its endorsement of AR-210-10. Secretary of War Henry Stimson specifically declared that no longer could separation of military personnel be based on race in the use of facilities, including officers' clubs.[18]

The dissident black officers were overjoyed and had an especially good party off base that night; no one had expected the ordeal to be over in such a short time. As for General Hunter, he blamed the War Department for taking its orders from Eleanor Roosevelt.[19]

The problem of the 477th's fighting efficiency continued, however, despite the civil rights victory. With the outcome of the war in the Pacific still uncertain and the morale of the 477th at a low point, air corps leadership hastily called on

Colonel Benjamin O. Davis, Jr., and his black officers rotating from Europe to set up an all-black command structure for the 477th in June 1945.[20] Thus the air corps once again resorted to segregation as its weapon to handle racial disorder. But even as the 477th became known as "Ben Davis's air force," with its personnel exclusively made up of blacks, it represented for most black officers a vast improvement over what they had known, and their attitudes improved quickly.[21]

Colonel Ben Davis would serve as commander of the black fliers from the aftermath of the "Freeman Field mutiny" to the end of segregation and disappearance of the "black air force" in the spring of 1949. He was a very intelligent, dignified leader who personified military bearing; in a group photograph of the officers of the 477th, he was the soldier who sat uncompromisingly upright.[22] His ability to lead as a warrior went unquestioned; the Tuskegee Airmen had performed at their best in combat in the European theater when he was giving the commands. In peacetime he also would earn recognition as a superior leader. Despite the fact that he publicly stated his opposition to segregation in the service, Colonel Davis was determined that if a segregated command were necessary, his would be first class.[23] The men under him respected Davis for being "as military as any other leader of his rank," and they knew he was respected by many of the higher-ups.[24] In the wake of the Freeman Field episode black aviators in the 477th welcomed Colonel Davis's leadership enthusiastically, because they knew that they once again would be called upon to prove themselves and that Davis's professionalism would help them succeed.

It would not be an easy time for those in command, despite relocation to Lockbourne Army Air Field near Columbus, Ohio, in 1946. Lockbourne had excellent runways, hangar space, and good housing, but the black flying units stationed there were made to feel like pariahs in the wake of the "mutiny." They had gone to Lockbourne largely because they were not accepted anywhere else and even in Columbus their reception was mixed.[25] The editor of the *Columbus Citizen*

Colonel Benjamin O. Davis, Jr., who commanded black flyers in segregated commands in World War II and thereafter until desegregation in 1948. Davis would later retire from the air force as a lieutenant general.

objected that "this was still a white man's country" and called the black fliers a "bunch of troublemakers." He objected as well to United States "servants" being entrusted with the responsibility to fight for America. Reaction against the presence of black airmen at other places had been so intense that Davis had given orders to his men not even to talk about Lockbourne, and no one from the command was allowed to visit the base prior to relocation. When members of the 477th made their first flyover, they did so at 18,000 feet and in flights of fours for fear of "alarming the people."[26] There were other reasons to be discouraged. Officers of the 477th who wished to remain in the service were fighting for their jobs as the services cut back; they were forced to be very competitive for the small number of slots for black officers who sought regular army commissions, hence a status that assured them a longer tenure in the service. Conversations at the bachelor officer quarters at this time inevitably turned to uncertainty about chances for survival. The black aviators also were incensed over their inability to win promotions and the fact that officers' ranks at Lockbourne were well below authorization. For example, one fighter squadron was supposed to have had a lieutenant colonel and a major, yet its highest rank was captain. But there would be no more demonstrations. It was one thing to fight against clear-cut inequities under law, another to protest economic inequalities at a time when most officers were trying desperately to remain in military service where income still would be better than opportunities in civilian life.[27]

Despite the scarcity of promotions, Lieutenant James could not permit himself to despair for the future. At a time when most of his fellow officers were wondering what they would do after resigning from the service, he calmly stated to a group of officers preparing alternative careers, "Fellows, that is your affair. I am staying in and I expect to make general."[28] His need for leadership and recognition surfaced immediately at Lockbourne. Around base, on the ground, and in the air, he was known as a "hard charger." As one squadron mate recalled, "He was a focal point. People coalesced around him." On the base football team Chappie was a standout, playing his best ball against Ohio colleges; in the gym he was captain of one of the pick-up teams; and he led the parades the same way he led in the flight formations. He also quickly won a reputation as one of the best pilots at Lockbourne, a tribute that was confirmed by a young navy man who "hopped" a ride with James from Lockbourne to Langley Field in Virginia under extremely bad flying conditions. Years later the enlisted man recalled the experience: "During one period the treetops could only have been a few feet away. In fact, I think we touched a few, causing the crewchief to bring word from the cockpit that all was well because Lieutenant James was going up into the weather and he was at his best when using instruments." He lauded James as the "perfect pilot" for averting what seemed like certain disaster.[29]

Although a fighter pilot by temperament, Lieutenant James was forced ("it made me sick") to fly twin-engine bombers in the early years at Lockbourne, but he mastered the plane, becoming proficient enough to serve as an instrument check pilot for instructors for the B-25s.[30] And sometimes he handled the bigger plane as if it were a fighter. In fact, James's need to perform extraordinarily was so insistent it could result in danger to others as well as himself. One afternoon he chided his copilot in a B-25, "This plane should be capable of more than what a manufacturer describes. Let's give it a try." With that the two piloted a slow roll (a complete turnover). The bomber survived, but that maneuver was contrary to regulations because it was hazardous. On the other hand, Chappie's skill with a variety of planes explains why Colonel Davis selected Chappie as his copilot when he was first learning to fly bombers at Lockbourne, and why many younger pilots turned to him for advice. Somehow, others assumed that "if he were confronted with a problem it would straighten out."[31]

At times James's need for mastery and his need to be in the limelight produced near-disasters, an example being the summer day in 1947 at Eglin Field in Florida when he was being checked out in the P-47. (Fliers in the 477th were trained as

pilots in both fighters and bombers after June 1945). The
runway was short and landings on hot days were complicated
by thermals that kept planes up, seemingly floating. A
number of pilots were standing near the runway as James's
P-47 came in for a landing. An operations officer noted that
James was coming in high and he feared a crash. He ordered
Chappie, via the tower, to "take it around—try another
time," but James replied, "Don't worry I can handle it."
When Chappie was still aloft at the midpoint of the runway,
the officer again requested that he not try to land at that
instant but that he take the plane up and try again later; when
the officer received word that the pilot was still intent on
landing, he ordered firetrucks to the scene. Chappie had in
fact run out of landing space, but he still brought the plane
down, the engine finally cutting off in a giant sand dune at the
end of the runway. The plane was upside down, its wheels
spinning and Lieutenant James sitting in the canopy held in
place by its belts. When the pilots from his squadron rushed
to his side to remove him from the plane, he declared with a
boyish grin, "I thought I could make it."[32]

Lieutenant James was not content with being a conspicuous daredevil pilot and stalwart athlete at Lockbourne; he
was so avid for applause that he also became a master of
ceremonies for a series of smart talent shows on base, serving also as producer and occasional singer.[33] Audience response was favorable enough that Air Force Special Services
became interested and asked Chappie to put his production
on the road with talent from other air bases as well. It came to
be known as "Operation Happiness" and toured nationally in
1947–1948 with James as general manager, casting director,
and emcee. The shows received nationwide publicity, which,
of course, helped Chappie's popularity. He also supported
civil rights by refusing to hold separate performances for
blacks and whites in southern cities near air bases.[34]

Chappie James enjoyed the recognition he received from
his fellow pilots for being a natural leader, but he thirsted for
official acknowledgment of his ability while still mired in the

lowly rank of lieutenant. Although he admired the ability and success of Colonel Davis, he resented being kept at a first lieutenant's rank for five years, and he may have held Ben Davis personally responsible for that fact.[35] While the relationship between the two, both to become generals, would remain formally correct and outwardly pleasant, there were acute personality differences between them. Ben Davis was a taciturn, conservative, and proper officer who was raised by his father, the first black general officer in the army, to achieve success as an officer by strict military professionalism. Davis could only have winced at some of James's idiosyncrasies. Chappie had a reputation as a party goer and as a popular man with women for his story telling and singing. He was too offhand as well, allowing the crew in the flight line to call him Chappie and buzzing a mink ranch and destroying a litter of young mink, which, upon complaint of the rancher, forced the colonel to fine the lieutenant.[36] And the singing and dancing on stage must have caused Davis to wonder whether James would ever really become a soldier. But as events would soon determine, Ben Davis would have no authority over Chappie James's future.

While a few key officers on the staff of Lieutenant General Idwal H. Edwards, air force deputy chief of staff for personnel, had come to recognize by 1948 that segregation was infeasible—it prevented blacks from working at the higher efficiency levels of most white units, led to duplication and inefficient use of specialists, and would become inoperative in combat because of insufficient qualified replacements—the service could not muster determination to end the system until it was supplied by President Truman's Executive Order 9981 on July 26, 1948. When the air force received that directive to foster opportunities in the armed services, it acted with remarkable speed and resolution, completing the process of integrating blacks effectively within one year, at least three years before the army came to grips with the same problems.[37]

Stuart Symington, air force secretary, exerted decisive influence to hasten implementation. From border cities of Baltimore and later St. Louis, Symington, as a manager of the Emerson Radio Corporation Plant in St. Louis, had pioneered in integrating work facilities and expanding opportunities for black workers.[38] As Eugene Zuckert, then assistant secretary for the air force, recalled, Symington was "a very, very persuasive person." He got "General Edwards, his Deputy Chief of Personnel, and me and he told us he wanted this to happen, the President ordered this to happen and it was going to happen because it was right and because he [the President] said so, and he made Edwards the focal point from the military standpoint and me as his representative to see that it got done."[39] Symington himself told the generals if they didn't agree with his policy of integration they should resign as "we don't want it done halfway," and that clinched it.[40] The effectiveness of the integration owed much as well to the resolve of senior officers to explain the process throughout the service. Lieutenant General Daniel James later recalled that any officers who hoped to frustrate air force policy were aware that they risked serious consequences from senior commanders if they did not comply.[41]

One of the casualties of integration was, of course, "Ben Davis's air force" at Lockbourne. Black fliers no longer would experience either the inferiority or the protection that went with segregation. They would be screened and reassigned, mostly along the line of their specialities, with only a few surviving as fighter pilots.[42]

Colonel Davis nominated only his best pilots and those most likely to succeed emotionally to join white flying units.[43] It had been estimated that only about twelve of the Tuskegee Airmen would remain as fighter pilots (there had been approximately sixty fighter pilots at Lockbourne), roughly the number of blacks that would serve as fliers in the Korean War.[44] Thus James broke away from most of his black contemporaries who would pursue different career lines in the air force. Being a fighter pilot with all the visibility and bluster associated with that skill probably gave James an edge in promotions over the other blacks who failed to qualify. Remaining in operations also would help James secure promotions more rapidly than Lockbourne's field grade officers (majors or above), twelve in number, all of whom went into staff assignments or to schools after integration.[45] From this group only Colonel Davis later would emerge as a general along with James. As for the small number of blacks remaining in fighter planes, James would soon also outstrip them in rank because of his superior leadership skills, qualities he already had demonstrated in their company at Lockbourne.

The Tuskegee Airmen were now off to the four winds; for Chappie James this meant that he would, at last, have an opportunity to achieve rank and recognition commensurate with his capabilities. But, of course, it also meant that he now would have to confront squarely and surmount the barrier of the nation's racial prejudice as it manifested itself in the military.

4. Korea

The Eighteenth Fighter Group, Lieutenant James's first integrated unit, was based at Clark Air Force Base, sixty-five
miles north of Manila in the Philippines. At Clark, in 1949,
James would begin his career in the "white air force," his
popularity and respect, annual evaluation and promotion
being dependent thereafter almost exclusively on white officers. Although this situation would work to his advantage
after the civil rights movement in the 1960s, he would succeed earlier entirely because of his unusual personality and
proficiency in spite of resistance over race and color. His
achievements with the Eighteenth Fighter Group in the Philippines and later in Korea after American forces were assigned to stem the North Korean invasion of the South
exemplified James's ability to overcome racial prejudice by
personal and professional skills.

Clark Air Force Base was located in a beautiful valley amid
abundant tropical greenery relieved by clusters of brown
thatched roofs of Filipino huts. The scene in 1949 was not as
tranquil as the touristic view suggested because Filipino
Communists, the Huks, were operating in the vicinity, the
crack of their small arms sometimes heard above sounds of
propeller-driven aircraft. But real war seemed far away for
the fliers at Clark who enjoyed the good duty on base. It was a
large place with long runways, permanent facilities, attractive quarters for married officers, and a big swimming pool.
The Eighteenth was a close-knit unit with free beer at the
"O" club on Friday nights, good skits and entertainment,

and a first-rate musical group led by First Lieutenant Claude "Spud" Taylor.[1]

"I never will forget," Chappie later recalled, "the first night I walked into the Officers' Club at Clark Air Force Base, and everything stopped with the music. The band got quiet, there were whispered conversations, and I could see the heads turn in my direction, and then one would nudge the one next to him to direct his attention to, 'Look who's coming to dinner.' We came in on Friday evening. They were having happy hour at the hospital club, which was very popular. I never will forget that as long as I live. It was almost comic. They couldn't have done it better if it had been a movie. Finally the noise level started to come up again, and the guy who finally turned out to be my best friend bounced down off the stage and said, 'Welcome to the club. My name is Spud Taylor, what's yours?' From then on we struck up a great friendship. He invited me over to his house afterwards to a party and that broke the ice for me." Reflecting on that incident later, he declared, "I came to compete on an equal basis, and if they were going to try to hinder me with racism I was going to overcome through the power of excellence that my mother taught me long ago."[2]

When the word first reached the Eighteenth that two blacks were joining as fliers, there were misgivings, especially among officers from the South. One southern woman, the wife of an officer, was overheard to say, "I'll be damned if I will ever have a nigger in my house!" but within a month she was entertaining Lieutenant James and his wife at dinner.[3] The other black officer did not fare as well. As an officer who served at Clark has observed, "After a month or so it would have taken an incredible bigot to dislike Chappie James."[4]

Chappie was acceptable to his fellow fighter pilots primarily because he established that he was entitled to membership in the group. Squadron records attest that James ranked second among eighteen pilots in the Twelfth Squadron of the Eighteenth Fighter Group in bombing accuracy in one test and had the finest average for rocket firing, five hits for five fired.[5] He also came to be recognized as one of the three or four best ground gunners in the squadron, winning his share of bets in competition for the most hits.[6]

Lieutenant James proved a good social companion as well and this also won him respect and friends among the other pilots. The squadron's basketball players lauded James for scoring thirty points in his first game. When the spring of 1950 came around he played first base on the squadron's softball team, not because he was a great fielder but because of "his tremendous spirit and the effect he had on the morale of the rest of the team." That team was undefeated when the Korean War broke out in June 1950. He also played golf and tennis; an incongruous picture of James at Clark Air Force Base shows him standing on a sunny day in air force uniform beside his teammates all in tennis shorts.[7] He was even helpful with the children of fellow officers, driving them around in a dilapidated jeep. One of his fellow officers recalls, "Chappie never asked for anything special; he just wanted to be one of the guys." James probably obtained his greatest satisfaction from association with Spud Taylor and his band. Spud was a pleasant, fun-loving fighter pilot and musician who liked Chappie's singing, and Chappie enjoyed singing so much that their close friendship was inevitable. The two became inseparable, almost like brothers.[8]

Spud helped Chappie with his one really serious problem during integration. The James family was not as readily accepted as Chappie had been. Dorothy was respected but remained, because of her quiet ways, somewhat withdrawn. But Danice, the James's oldest child, was going to kindergarten and she was badgered by other school children. Chappie described her predicament and Spud Taylor's help for his family as follows:

> She would go down to the corner to catch the bus with the kids, and they would walk over to the other side of the street. A lady came and asked them,

"Why do you do that? I've been watching you from
my house. (This happened to be Taylor's wife.)
Everytime she crosses over you run back. Why do
you do that to her?" One of these little girls, who
was obviously the leader, started looking around and
then said, "Well, uh, er, she's got a lunchbox and we
don't have one." And Mrs. Taylor said, "I don't
think that's the reason. I gave her the lunch box, and
I will give you all one. Then will you stand . . . ?"
"No, we are not going to stand with her because she
is a nigger." "Now who told you that?" "My daddy
and my mommy did, they told me that she is a
nigger."
Anyway, it worked out because Spud went down
and had a little talk with the mommies and daddies.[9]

Lieutenant James would remain loyal and grateful to his
dear friend. When his third child, a male, was born, Chappie
and Dorothy would name him Claude and his nickname
would be Spud.[10]
James missed no opportunity to be friendly or well-liked
by white officers and their families. His outgoing behavior
reflected his need for popular approval as well as his determination to establish that he was a social equal. As in every
other aspect of his early career, however, his sociability probably was motivated primarily by considerations of success.
As a black attempting to qualify in a white squadron he knew
that his future promotions would depend on the opinions of
white officers. Friends meant support and protection, recommendations, and advancement. In his obsessive quest for
personal recognition and success Chappie went so far as to
complain to white officers about the inadequate flying skills
and deficient personal behavior of the other black officer
assigned to the Eighteenth. Chappie was embarrassed because the deficiencies of that officer could lead to negative,
unwarranted stereotyping of all black fliers. Here again, as
was typical in his career, Chappie James assumed the posi-

tion of a black individualist rather than spokesman for black solidarity. Blacks who didn't perform well diluted the chances for others to succeed, himself included. Because he believed that the progress of the race depended on the personal strengths of its leaders, he had no problem justifying his criticism of an inferior black officer.

A major event of Lieutenant James's stay at Clark Air Force Base came during a crash just after takeoff in the spring of 1950. Flying in a two-seater T-33, he and a fellow pilot headed north from the air base and had a flameout at an altitude of fifty feet. Unable to restart in the short air time remaining, they steered the plane into a dry rice paddy, where it pancaked and came to a sliding stop. The crash knocked the pilot in the front seat unconscious. Because jet fuels are highly combustible under such conditions, James desperately sought to exit from the back seat, though the canopy could not be opened because the controls were in the front seat. He decided to rear back against the Plexiglas canopy and exert his powerful frame to loosen the pins that fastened the canopy. He succeeded, and he rescued the unconscious pilot in the front seat, a man who weighed over two hundred pounds, and dragged him to safety before the plane burned. The air force had assumed it was impossible for a man to exert that much force against such a strong locking system and to bend it. Chappie sustained severe burns and a bad back for which he was hospitalized for several weeks, but he also was awarded a Distinguished Service Medal for valor.[11]

While recuperating, Chappie and the members of his squadron were informed that North Koreans had crossed the South Korean border and that President Truman had ordered the air force into action against the aggressors. The Twelfth departed Clark Air Force Base on July 10 and went to Japan, where they were given World War II vintage Mustangs. By July 15 they were ready to join battle against what then seemed to be an invincible North Korean invader.[12] Lieutenant James, who was still convalescing, was forced to delay his departure for Japan and Korea for several weeks.[13]

The North Korean Army had launched an all-out attack against lightly armed South Korean defenders in the early hours of June 25, 1950, and it rapidly achieved victories, penetrating that day to within 17 miles of Seoul, the South Korean capital. The North Koreans' T-34 tanks, the same type that the Russians had used against crack German divisions, drove at will against poorly prepared South Korean units, while their Soviet-manufactured planes controlled the air and strafed and bombed South Korea's retreating soldiers and fleeing civilians. Within three days the fall of Seoul was imminent, and General Douglas MacArthur was warning Washington that there was danger of a complete collapse of the South Korean line. The North Korean Army was then only 150 miles from Pusan, the southernmost port in Korea and, if captured, the prize of all Korea as well as a threat to the American bases in Japan.

Despite the imminent dangers, American policy makers and hence the American military were at first slow to respond to the North Korean invasion.[14] On June 27, President Truman announced that American naval and air forces would assist the South Koreans; on June 30, with Seoul under assault, American ground troops were committed as well. Only one American division was at first assigned, the Twenty-fourth, and that comprised mostly young soldiers, many of them and their officers ill-prepared from indulgent living in Japan. Once committed to the engagement they were no match for the weapons or the determination of their adversaries. Recoilless rifles and bazookas could not stop the T-34s, the young American soldiers could not cope with their better-disciplined foe. More American troops would have to be assigned, but in the interim the defense line as of July 13 would be 60 miles south of Seoul and only 100 miles from Pusan. Meanwhile, clusters of frightened South Korean civilians passed through American lines, some of them walking, others with bikes, and others pushing carts with all their possessions on their backs; their retreat did nothing to improve the morale of young, outnumbered, and ill-equipped troops.[15]

There were many uncertain moments in the remainder of July and August, but the tide began to shift for American, Republic of Korea, and allied forces, now called United Nations forces, especially in August. Part of the explanation lay with the enemy's supply problems; North Korean tanks outran their sources of fuel and ammunition along Korea's rough and tortuous roads in mountain valleys. Another reason was, of course, quick and resourceful preparation of American troops for battle under the command of General MacArthur. As the North Koreans initiated what they hoped would be their victory assault, they were forced to do battle against an effective buildup of planes, weapons, and men in a sixty-mile square known as the Pusan perimeter.

American air power had proved decisive in stopping the North Korean advance. The first combat mission by the Twelfth Fighter-Bomber Squadron employed the effective Mustangs from a base near the battle front and, beginning July 15, provided a turning point in the air-ground offensive. (By August 11 they would be joined in Korea by five other Mustang [F-51] squadrons with 150 combat aviators, including Lieutenant Daniel James).[16] The Mustangs were better than jets (F-80s) for the type of continuous close ground support of United Nations troops required to counter the North Koreans. They required only short takeoff and landing space, hence were suited to the small and bumpy landing strips in Korea. And because they cruised at low air speeds and therefore consumed little fuel, they could cover battlefields for several hours at a time, meeting little opposition since the North Korean Air Force with its faster Yaks had been destroyed by U.S. Navy aircraft carrier pilots.[17] The Mustang carried six machine guns, rockets, and two 500-pound bombs or napalm; it was a lethal aerial platform when used efficiently. In late July and early August, when the out-

come of the conflict was most uncertain, the Mustangs operated against the North Koreans like airborne artillery, head
on and point blank, sometimes as low as ten feet above the
ground and only fifty feet in front of U.N. lines. When the
North Koreans kept coming, menacing the air base from
which the Twelfth flew its missions, the U.S. fliers aban-
doned base in Korea and flew from Japan. On September 7,
they returned to the Korean mainland when base K-9,
dubbed Dogpatch by the fliers, was opened to them near
Pusan, at the same time that the North Koreans mounted
their major attack on the Pusan perimeter.[18]

With the battlefield only fifteen minutes away from K-9,
each fighter pilot flew five to eight missions a day. Bombs,
rockets, and rounds were stacked hurriedly in piles on the
airfield, each plane taxiing to each point of installation. Pilots
experienced intense physical and nervous strain; they were
exhausted from the effect of combat flying, the reloadings,
and the incredible heat that sucked oxygen from the narrow
cockpit of the Mustang.[19]

In the end, it was the Mustang pilots who punished the
North Koreans so badly that they no longer could move
forward. From an altitude of 2,000 feet, where the strafing
run began, they went down to treetop levels. They freed
American troops when they were surrounded and stopped
North Korean attacks before they could start. At times the
strafing became complicated, especially when the North
Koreans dressed like fleeing South Korean civilians, with
whom they mingled, concealing weapons under their white
pajamas. But the Mustangs mainly concentrated on trains
and trucks and tanks and interdicted the enemy's operational
support. Flights of two or four planes were used, with a low-
flying plane looking for camouflaged vehicles. Once this pilot
sighted the vehicles, which usually were betrayed by muzzle
flashes, the others would converge to destroy the supply
column. The Mustang pilots also kept supply trains bottled
up in tunnels for days until one of them found a way to dive in
and slide a napalm bomb into the entrance and then pull out

quickly. These types of actions by Mustang pilots explain why North Korean prisoners of war revealed that tactical air power contributed substantially to the demoralization and defeat of their army.[20]

Chappie James, after his arrival in early August, was performing these types of missions enthusiastically. His old friends, Lieutenant Claude "Spud" Taylor and Lieutenant Howard C. "Scrappy" Johnson, a teammate from softball at Clark Air Force Base, had requested of their commanding officer that Chappie be assigned to their flight.[21] He agreed and the "ferocious four" became a fighting unit and an inseparable social group: Ted "Mother" Baader, who liked to look after the others; Spud Taylor, a sax player; Scrappy Johnson, an English major from the University of Louisville who had had the temerity to go out for varsity football there despite his modest 5'8", 150-pound build; and Chappie. They flew everyday together in August and September, and once each week they visited the hospital club in Pusan to drink beer because there was none at K-9. When Mother Baader got feisty there one night with a marine officer who told them the air force couldn't fly as well as marines, Chappie and Scrappy restrained him from punching the offender. And when Chappie was baptized a Catholic (his mother was a convert to Catholicism at this time), Mother Baader stood as his godfather.[22] Because they got along so well, they took turns as flight leader and, because Chappie frequently had declared to them his pride in his black American heritage, when it was Chappie's turn he was "Black Leader" on radio and his flight was called the "Black Flight." Chappie also sported a black panther insignia on his flight helmet, a sign of his continuing pride in the Tuskegee Airmen and his identification with them.[23]

Chappie was leading the flight on October 15, 1950—one month after General MacArthur had executed his brilliant amphibious flanking operations against the North Koreans at Inchon, leading to their retreat from the Pusan perimeter—

when he earned the Distinguished Flying Cross. The citation that noted his recent promotion to captain read in part:

Captain James displayed outstanding airmanship and aeronautical skill when he led a flight of four (4) F-51 type fighter aircraft on a mission in support of United Nations' ground forces near Namchonjom, Korea. Directed to the target by friendly artillery spotter shells, Captain James led a series of devastating attacks with napalm, rockets, and machine gun fire against enemy positions only a few yards from friendly troops. Despite a visibility restricted by dense haze and smoke and a determined barrage of anti-aircraft and automatic weapons fire, this officer continued his attacks until all ammunition was expended. Captain James personally killed over one hundred (100) enemy troops. As a result of this highly successful mission, the enemy suffered heavy casualties and was forced to withdraw from an attack on friendly ground forces. By his high personal courage and devotion to duty, Captain James has brought great credit upon himself, and the United States Air Force.[24]

At the time of Chappie's distinguished mission, the Twelfth already had lost four pilots (missing in action) out of twenty-six flying with the unit; it would go on to suffer nine more fatalities in the next five months.[25] Because enemy air action was virtually nonexistent until the Chinese moved in with force in December 1950, planes were lost largely through machine gun and small arms fire when they strafed at low levels; the F-51 engine used liquid coolant and a machine gun bullet in the radiator could bring down the plane. Every mission that required low-level passes or strafing was therefore very dangerous. The danger was compounded because the North Koreans were known to have executed American pilots who were shot down, and American recovery operations at this time, before helicopters (choppers) had range, were not effective. Downed pilots were left entirely to their own resources and no one from the Twelfth who was shot down was ever recovered. In early November in the mid-part of the Korean peninsula as U.N. forces drove north to the Chinese border, Spud Taylor was hit and downed. He was covering a parachute drop of American troops to release American prisoners of war about ten miles behind the battle lines. He was able to remove himself from the plane and crawl into a ditch where he lay, presumably, with a broken leg. Chappie took over the flight and he and the others circled the spot giving cover with their machine guns. When Spud was sighted, Chappie called on the radio for a helicopter and gave Spud's location. He was informed that all choppers were on an alert to offer protection to General MacArthur, who was being flown over the battlefield that day. Chappie became exasperated and flew to the chopper base while the F-51s continued to cover Spud. Chappie demanded that one chopper be released to recover Spud, but he was unsuccessful. The next day, army units occupying the place where the Mustangs had circled found Spud's body riddled with bullets.[26]

James had flown about sixty-five dangerous missions when Spud was shot down. He had nightmares for a long time thereafter and went into a deep depression. James's devotion to "the power of excellence" had carried him far, but the strain of combat and now the loss of his closest friend brought him close to a breakdown. He was given rest and relaxation in Japan; his commanding officer was concerned that otherwise he would be unable to fly. When he returned to Korea, Chappie was reassigned to flying the little T-6 spotting plane and later, as he felt better, to dangerous photo-reconnaissance operations in an unarmed reconnaissance jet over North Korea. He completed these assignments and returned after one hundred total missions to Clark Air Force Base in the Philippines.[27]

Chappie James returning from mission in Korea, 1950.
(Courtesy of U.S. Air Force)

Chappie never discussed the setback to his ideals of fear-lessness and mastery. It may have been a bitter and difficult time for him, but it is more likely that he repressed the experi-ence and assumed, as he did when he failed to make the football team in high school, that it really did not happen or at least not in such a way that it impaired his image as a master-ful person. Later he would enlarge on his accomplishments in Korea, describing himself as having "established [there] a professional reputation as an outstanding fighter pilot."[28] If his overstatement was compensatory, he may have been un-consciously merciful to himself because he had acquitted himself well in a difficult air war.

5. As a Leader

Chappie James made rapid progress in rank and status after Korea; he became a major in 1952 and a lieutenant colonel in 1956. Of the six black fighter pilots who would become generals by the time of James's death in 1978 only Benjamin O. Davis, Jr., had moved up more rapidly, in part because his promotions were facilitated by World War II and the U.S. Army Air Corps's dependency on him, a West Point graduate, to command the segregated black fliers.[1] In April 1953, Major James became the first black officer to command a fighter squadron in the American Defense Command, and all the pilots under him were white.[2] This fact established that he had distinguished himself from the surviving black fighter pilots after the integration of pilots at Lockbourne. At that time James's commanding officer (wing commander) at Otis Air Force Base described him "as our outstanding pilot, a born leader and good guy. Discipline and efficiency are high in his squadron, maybe because he never expects his boys to do anything he can't do himself and better." Before long the 437th under Major James recorded the fastest turn-around time for squadrons in the annual air defense exercises on the eastern seaboard and later defeated all neighboring squadrons in rocketry as well.[3] As a consequence of these and other achievements, James was promoted while at Otis AFB in Massachusetts to the rank of lieutenant colonel. The air force then signaled that James had a special future in the service by assigning him from Otis to its Command and Staff College, which emphasized leadership skills, and then to the

Pentagon. In 1962 at forty-two years of age James was assigned as squadron commander at one of the country's most important overseas air bases, Royal Air Force Bentwaters, England, where swift fighter-bombers had been fitted out with a nuclear capability. Within a year he was promoted to deputy commander of wing operations at Bentwaters and was responsible for the pilot training and proficiency of fliers in all the fighter squadrons on base.[4] Clearly, he had received repeated votes of confidence from the air force and was within reach of becoming a general officer with only two more promotions required and eleven years remaining before thirty years of service and probable retirement.

James's rise was partially attributable to the fact that the air force had by the mid-1960s "moved well beyond the formalities of integration" to a degree "seldom found in other major institutions of American society."[5] This is not to say that promotions for black officers were wholly equitable then. Particular commanders still manifested covert prejudice by preferring whites over blacks, regardless of abilities, for positions that led to promotion, such as operations officer or flight leader. Much also depended on what commanders wrote on each officer's evaluations, which permitted latitude for racial discrimination. James had experienced his share of disappointments over racial issues, especially on his first assignment after the Korean War to a base near Rome, New York, where a biased squadron commander deliberately tried to make James uncomfortable and boasted he would find ways to get him out of the unit.[6] Reassignment to Otis AFB on Cape Cod also presented its problems when Chappie and his family were, for racial reasons, denied rental homes in a select area. Years later he would say about the incident, "That's a sore spot. That's a very sore spot."[7] And there were still the embarrassments of overnight traveling in the South and in moving about in Montgomery, Alabama, where James attended the Command and Staff College at Maxwell AFB just after the Montgomery bus boycott in the mid-1950s. The tensions in the surrounding community caused James to prefer to remain on base.[8] James had coped with earlier disappointments over racial prejudice in the air force and in off-base circumstances like housing and recreation in a variety of ways depending on the severity of the issue and, of course, his ability to effect change. He eliminated many possible occasions of prejudice in persons whom he contacted, both military and civilian, by his personal dignity, ability, and humor, just as he had done in Korea. He also consciously sought to counteract prejudice by public service.[9] His youth work and public speaking among youth in the vicinity of Otis AFB led to great public favor and his selection as Young Man of the Year in 1954 by the Massachusetts Chamber of Commerce, an award that doubtless helped his service career.[10] He also gave pep talks to high school football teams, which led to a unique relationship with a white player of Portuguese-American background, Gerry Cardozzo. Although many of James's public initiatives outside the air force probably represented inseparable motivations of generosity and self-interest, his regard for Gerry, almost wholly a private relationship, expressed a different facet of his personality. Gerry's opportunities appeared to be severely limited because his family could not afford to send him to college. Chappie drew on his friends at the predominantly black college, Florida A & M, and helped secure a full athletic scholarship for Gerry; James also paid Gerry's bus fare to Tallahassee, Florida. When Gerry protested he could never repay these favors, Chappie replied, "When you get in the same position someday, help someone else." The two would remain close while Gerry played football at A & M, James flying to visit him during football season and helping Gerry with transportation costs between Massachusetts and Florida, with a stopover in Washington, D.C., while Chappie was there. Indeed, Chappie often introduced Gerry with great affection as another of his sons.[11] In the process, of course, James also was declaring, whether consciously or not, that he was qualified (i.e., like any white person) to assume responsibility "to adopt" and help a young man regardless of the color differences between them. While James exercised diplomacy and skill in dispelling racial stereotypes in his personal relationships, he also could be outspoken when he personally encountered institutional discrimination, and he worked forthrightly to eliminate discriminatory practices still affecting blacks in the armed services. He was largely responsible for integrating golf courses (golf was his favorite hobby) in the immediate vicinity of Otis AFB, and he accompanied Representative Charles C. Diggs, Jr., a fellow Tuskegee Airman, on the latter's inspection of racial complaints in the Pacific in 1959, a mission that helped to reactivate the President's Commission on Civil Rights in the Armed Forces under John F. Kennedy.[12] At the same time, however, James avoided identification with movements or protests on behalf of black causes in civilian society, such as the bus boycott. He believed that blacks could best be helped socially by demonstrating that able and disciplined blacks could succeed. James knew that his becoming a general could do much for the image of blacks and for their practical well-being in the military service, and he chose not to compromise his chances through political activism with questionable results.[13]

James's rapid rise in rank was unique among his contemporaries, the black fighter-pilot officers who trained at Tuskegee. The explanation for his success lies not merely with an improving racial egalitarianism in the air force, but in Chappie's will to establish his equality, if not superiority, through his proficiency, hence to force the system to prove itself equitable. Recognition and rewards were conferred on him primarily because of his effectiveness as a leader. In the process of establishing his qualifications James exerted himself to the fullest, or, as one of his contemporaries at Bentwaters noted, "Chappie got on his horse and rode off at full speed in four different directions. He did everything at full speed."[14] Yet James was never quite sure, despite chronic hypertension, whether he was doing enough, and he continued to quote his mother's maxims to his fellow officers to justify that he and they try even harder.[15]

Lieutenant Colonel James's style of leadership was quite different from the one employed by Colonel Robin Olds, Chappie's commanding officer and the wing commander of Eighty-first Tactical Fighter Wing stationed at RAF Bentwaters. Olds was respected, even revered, by the eighty fighter pilots at Bentwaters. He had been an All-American tackle at West Point in 1942, an ace and hero in World War II, having accounted for the destruction of thirteen German planes, and he had married a movie star, Ella Raines.[16] But for Olds, leadership began at the flight line. While Olds deservingly had won and would rewin in Vietnam title to being an outstanding combat fighter pilot, his talks to the fliers on base often left men feeling a little uneasy, as if something were tentative. By comparison James was an expert ground commander. As one young pilot recalled, Chappie James's briefings to his fliers every morning were "so great. They reminded me of what I would imagine to be the effect of a Notre Dame locker room at halftime. He made you think that dropping the practice bomb that day was the most important thing you did in your whole life. He would relate it to national security, defense, the threat from the Russians or whatever else gave you pride in performing your mission well." James led by his ability "to make fliers chomp at the bit to fire the nearest rocket or drop the closest bomb."[17]

James's size—6'4", 250 pounds—unquestionably contributed to his ability to command. As a contemporary at Bentwaters observed, "'My God,' they would say, 'look at that massive appearance!'" Chappie caught people's attention and held it with dramatic movements and articulate speech. But it was his ability to inspire and to convince that made him unique for his times. Few officers at RAF Bentwaters better understood how to reach their personnel and fewer still how to motivate them. They undoubtedly shared his patriotism and his positive ethic, but they could not articulate these attitudes as convincingly. As a result, "no one else could get the morale going in an outfit overall as Chappie."[18]

James exerted this kind of leadership without provoking resentment for being black because he minimized racial factors with a type of humanity that caused whites to focus on his character, not his color. He consciously deflated the differences that color made, avoided separatism, and was free from reverse racism. He attempted to de-emphasize race by joshing with vernacular references to "niggers" and "honkies." At times, he told his fellow officers he was BNIC (Big Nigger in Charge). To others, who protested he had not called lately, he might reply, "I'm sorry, but I haven't revised my honkie list lately." Another favorite when he couldn't remember someone was, "Oh, all you white guys look alike to me."[19]

Chappie's sensitivity to the needs of others was at the heart of his successful leadership in other ways. He especially understood the needs and feelings of subordinates for recognition and friendship. Typically, when Captain Ed Orr, a physician and recent graduate of the University of Mississippi Medical School, arrived at Bentwaters without his young bride because he had no housing in England and because her transportation was complicated by passport regulations, Orr was astonished to find one of his first callers was James, a squadron commander, assuring him that he would see to it that these problems were worked out quickly. Orr reflected later, "His call was typical of his going the extra mile to make you feel part of the team."[20]

James's skills in personnel management showed in other ways as well. He spent many hours making the work of fliers as pleasant as possible. He inspected the quality of food served to them, and if they were coming in from a late night mission he would meet them. He inquired into the adequacy of living quarters for the enlisted men, and he inspected stoves in their work areas. He befriended others by being tolerant toward first offenders. Captain William J. Baugh once flipped up his fuel probe in front of the windscreen of the F-101A to give a finger to the other fliers taxiing on the runway. He forgot to depress the probe, and he got a low fuel signal and was forced to land prematurely, damaging the plane. He went to Lieutenant Colonel James and explained his mistake, the operations director's reply being simply, "Hey, that wasn't too bright," and Chappie had a friend for life.[21] James drew the line for repeated offenders, however. They were obstructionists who hurt the unit's efficiency, and he treated them disdainfully. This same principle governed his response to racial conflicts on base, for which his prestige and mediatory skills often were solicited. He refused to carry weaklings, regardless of race. Although he was respected by black enlisted personnel, they found, perhaps to their discomfort, they could not count on his unconditional favor. He was apt to say to them, "You've got the talent. Stop complaining and do something to help yourself."[22]

While Chappie led from a broad base, he relied heavily, in fact indispensably, on the tight-knit support of a loyal band of perhaps fifteen friends. They were essential to his management efficiency and important to his social life and personal pleasure, but they were best understood as Chappie James's "family" because initiation into that circle meant a degree of intimacy, cooperation, and loyalty usually reserved for conventional family life.[23]

Chappie chose his family carefully. The first and most essential requirement was that members accept him as leader. If an officer had similar aspirations he was better off alone or in his own group because James relished being called "Chief" on the job and was a limelight person socially. He also demanded that members of his family perform competently, with the kinds of skills to assure that they could fulfill requirements of the organization (and Chappie's command) effectively. James sought out effective people as his close friends because they became his aides-de-camp, but it was not enough that they perform well and reflect well on James. It was also critical that they show loyalty and affection to him in return for his commitments to them. James reciprocated these favors with good duty assignments, recommendations for advancement, and inclusion in his intimate social groups. One final attribute cemented the family. Chappie liked to drink "deep-dish olive pies" (Beefeater martinis), and with the gin flown in from Malta at very cheap costs (two dollars a fifth) the group often partied together. The family then became exuberant and drank and socialized with the "Chief" until the early morning. As one member of the family remarked on recollection, "We loved one another as much as any group of men can love."[24]

Ed Orr, the air force physician from Mississippi, belonged to Chappie's family. He was impressed by the personal courage and skill of single-seater fighter pilots, who hurled their bodies at the ground day after day, and by their nonchalant code of bravery. Furthermore, he relished camaraderie and the antics at Chappie's parties. But he also enjoyed being the physician for James's squadron, all the more because the air force did not officially assign doctors to squadrons. The "Chief" had made up bogus orders for him in jest, however, and Orr attended all the squadron meetings as if he were a pilot. James had shown Orr that he deserved to be included with fliers and Orr's presence at the meetings, inasmuch as it was unprecedented for doctors to attend, reassured fliers and their families of James's personal interest in them.

Major Ralph Maglione, who would retire from the air force as a two-star general, was Chappie's closest friend—a Kent State graduate, handsome, dapper, and an outstanding pilot who would later captain the air force aerobatic team, the Thunderbirds. "Maggie" was close to Chappie because he filled all the requirements; very competent and yet a team player under Chappie and an entertainer and party goer. Some of the performances by the two on the bar in the officers' club at Bentwaters or at Wheelus Air Force Base in Libya, where the Eighty-first Wing would go to fly for better weather, were legendary. For example, Chappie sang "Sonny Boy" to Maggie, who was sitting on his lap wearing a blue bonnet, and their audience became hilarious at the incongruous sight. Chappie then delivered a few ethnic jokes aimed at Italians, and Maggie replied, "Did you hear about those two new hotels they are building in town, the 'Coonrad Hilton' and 'Niggerbocker'?" Or he ribbed Chappie about his two new cars, "his Falcoon and Jiguar."[25]

Captain Bill Kirk, also later to be a general, would not seem a likely candidate for James's inner circle. He had enlisted in the air force and had not attended college, and he lacked glamour and theatrics, characteristics of the fraternity. But he had "great hands" and a feel for an airplane like few others, so much so that he and Robin Olds flew in a class by themselves. When Chappie flew at night, something he was reluctant to do, Bill Kirk usually flew his wing and served as his eyes. Kirk was also loyal to James in other ways, and the "Chief," according to Kirk, reciprocated "with an understanding of loyalty as no one I had ever met."[26] Chappie later "proved his friendship [for Kirk] over and over," including the time in Vietnam when Kirk received word his father was ill. James cut all red tape to assure Kirk's swift departure from base, and he arranged for a C-47 to fly Kirk to Saigon, where he made direct connections to San Francisco. James also arranged for an F-4 to be at the commercial airport in San Francisco to take Kirk immediately to the vicinity of his home.[27]

Lieutenant Colonel Ed Rischer from Louisiana belonged to the select group because he and James worked well together. Rischer was maintenance officer of the wing and was responsible for servicing the planes used by James's fliers; he was, therefore, in a position to affect decisively the quality of James's job performance. Although a maintenance officer's relationship to a director of operations is often uneasy, James's and Rischer's cooperation led to the wing's winning awards for having all planes and pilots in action for operational readiness tests. The two were also close off-duty friends. They were neighbors in the same red and white Tudor duplex on base, and James came to be addressed as "Uncle Chappie" in the Rischer household, a sign of their affection for him. Years later when the two were serving in separate commands and one of Rischer's sons was killed in an accident, Chappie, then a three-star general, flew to Florida to spend a day with Rischer. Even after Ed Rischer retired from the service, James continued to call him once or twice a month mostly about family and personal matters.[28]

While most officers at RAF Bentwaters, those in the special circle and those not so close to Chappie, recognized his human frailties, his extraordinary ambition, his politicking (he spent "a lot of time on the phone making friends"), his adroit manipulation and insatiable need to be at the center of things with a team revolving around him, their fondness for him was not diminished. As one flier, not a close friend, recalls, "Everyone liked him. He was like John F. Kennedy; nobody wanted to find fault with him."[29]

RAF Bentwaters had a reputation among American fliers for generating an exceptionally active social life in after-duty hours. The good times were actually a reaction to the hard work of the base; normal workdays for fliers lasted more than ten hours, with sixteen to seventeen hours not uncommon. The perils of flying the F-101A also contributed a hell-may-care quality to off-duty life. Between January 1961 and January 1963 the wing lost four of its seventy-five fighter pilots. One, Lieutenant Raymond Nishibayashi, experienced a hard "nose-over" at 2,000 feet. His plane hit the water before the pilot could eject or recover from his spin. An F-101A with Lieutenant Roger Bye emerged almost vertically from the overcast at a very high speed. Ejection from the cockpit succeeded, but Bye apparently failed to reckon his altimeter correctly and catapulted from the plane too late. He was crushed on impact.[30] Lieutenant Sterling Lee's plane stalled out on a turning final while approaching the runway. He bailed out, but his body was pulverized into mush on the concrete below.[31] Visibility, which was typically abominable (400 feet below and one mile ahead), contributed to accidents as well. One pilot, Captain Houghton Reed, flying in exceptionally rough weather, twenty-five miles off course, hit a mountain peak in Scotland. When three fighter pilots and a flight surgeon went out to make an accident report, they found his remains beside the charred plane: shoes with a toe in one of them and piece of flesh in a trouser leg.[32]

The fighter pilots had coping systems for these awful facts of their working lives. Their magnificent egos provided the first defense; they reasoned that accidents just didn't happen—at least silly accidents didn't happen to really good fliers. To the sinister thought that it could happen on a fateful day to anyone, most would respond that they might be severely tested on occasion but they would recover and later order free beer at the officers' club for everyone and have a great indestructible laugh together. Fast cars and attractive women were also major consolations for the dangers of flying. Exchange rates for Americans in Great Britain were excellent in the early 1960s, the result being a profusion of Porsches, Ferraris, Mercedes, and even Jaguars in parking areas near Bentwaters. Women quickly assembled once they heard about a party for fighter pilots. The parties began with innocent chatter and the clamor of ice cubes and ended according to very personal standards. Whether an officer was married or single was not as important on a particular evening as whether he was handsome and danced well. The rationalization was that the 1960s was a time when everybody was trying something new, anyway, so a party of mixed marrieds and singles did not seem so objectionable. Wives of officers were upset about these parties if they were living on base and heard reports, but more often they were back home in the United States.

Lieutenant Colonel James and his close friends were in the forefront socially. It was his ethic to do everything to the limit, both work and play, though the two were not to be mixed. Chappie formally endorsed the air force maxim, "He who hoots with the owls at night cannot fly with the eagle in the morning." Parties were sustenance to him, however; they provided an appreciative audience for his wit, dancing, and singing. His attitude toward women was no different from

that of most fliers, while women in England, with a freer
tradition of interracial socializing, often were fascinated by
him. When his wife was away in the States, Chappie sometimes sat in the officers' club and sighed when the lieutenants
and captains brought in their attractive companions. Occasionally he danced with an unmarried woman who came to
the club with another officer. When the same woman showed
up several more times and Chappie spent the evening dining,
drinking, and dancing with her, eyebrows were raised; it was
one thing to do this at a select party, another to do so in the
presence of all the officers and their wives on base at the
officers' club. But others perceived James's insistence on
displaying his right to enjoy the permissive moral climate at
Bentwaters, and to do so in the company of a white woman,
as a demonstration once again of his credo, which emphasized personal quality rather than color as the only legitimate
basis of entitlement.[33]

In these troublesome yet hopeful times for American
blacks in the mid-1960s, Lieutenant Colonel James was insistent on asserting his personal civil rights. When Robin Olds
suggested that James fly to Tucson (his duty after Bentwaters
was at nearby Davis-Monthan Air Force Base)[34] from Pensacola, Florida, rather than travel across the southern United
States by car, James replied, heatedly, "I intend to drive this
damn car [Jaguar] anywhere I want to go."[35] James applauded demonstrations as long as they were peaceful and
nonviolent, and he apparently even considered resigning his
commission over the ugly reaction to peaceful protest at
Selma, Alabama.[36] But he was also emphatic in his opposition to violent protest. In a speech at the Tucson Country
Club, Orr heard Chappie declare that "if anyone threw a
rock, [I] would be on the other side."[37] His statements were
reprinted in the *Chicago Sun,* prompting many irate letters
and phone calls from blacks and causing his wife Dorothy to
change their phone number to unlisted. Chappie was un-
happy because he found himself in the position of denounc-
ing other blacks, but that would remain his position.[38]

James's attitude toward black social protest movements in the 1960s was more conditional than his insistence on his own personal rights. James's background caused him to see social problems of blacks conservatively, in individual and characterological terms. He believed that blacks who accepted the challenge to develop to their fullest potential would overcome prejudice. For him the quest to establish that he was one of the best in his society became a heroic and romantic adventure. However, the effective new black protest movements in the United States prompted James to become more thoughtful of the social context of problems encountered by blacks. In part this awareness may have arisen from his being a beneficiary of that protest; some white officers even assumed that he now enjoyed official favor and perquisites because he was black. The new black civil rights leadership—especially Whitney Young (of the Urban League), Roy Wilkins (of the NAACP), and Martin Luther King, Jr.—also contributed to James's heightened sense of black solidarity. They stood for political and social change but did not believe in deliberately antagonizing the dominant white society. Their personal styles, speech, and education also approximated ideals that Chappie had been taught to respect as a child. He could appreciate the wisdom of King's dictum from Booker T. Washington, "Let no man pull you so low to make you hate him," and King's intent to bring increased dignity to black people in the United States. He also could respond affirmatively to King's message of faith in the future, education, and confidence in youth. But while Chappie now used the term "black" instead of "Negro" and supported law breaking when the law was discriminatory (such as laws forbidding peaceful demonstrations at Selma) and the validity of separate roads to cherished goals, he retained on an emotional level his commitment to individual excellence as the most viable course for the social amelioration of blacks. The success he began to experience in the 1960s and early 1970s would only confirm his adherence to that ethic.[39]

The big news at the crack fighter bases in the United States in 1965 was Vietnam. In March 1965 the United States decided to intervene there with the deployment of organized ground combat units and continuous bombing of North Vietnam. When the Viet Cong and North Vietnamese answered by escalating military action, U.S. leaders responded in kind. The Americans intended to punish the enemy on the ground and in the air to convince him that the Viet Cong could not win in the south. As part of that process, the air force stepped up operations from bases that the American government had negotiated with the government of Thailand. These provided close access to the Ho Chi Minh Trail in adjacent Laos, hence an opportunity to stymie the flow of goods and arms to the Viet Cong. The bases were also close enough to North Vietnam to permit attacks on its industrial areas from the west, thus compounding problems for enemy defenses that expected American planes from the south.

Colonel Robin Olds, who was assigned to take command of the base at Ubon, Thailand, visited Davis-Monthan in the summer of 1966 looking for volunteers to join his new fighter wing. His reputation as a leader was so outstanding that applicants kept calling to offer service. Many of them had flown the difficult F-101A at Bentwaters and now were skilled as instructors in the air forces' most advanced fighter, the F-4. Olds handpicked his outfit. To Chappie he said, "Last time I saw you, you were ten pounds overweight—if you lose it and want to fight, come on." To serve with Robin Olds at a time of war was the chance of a lifetime for a professional fighter pilot, and Chappie James, now a full colonel after a promotion at Davis-Monthan, wanted very much to go.[40] It meant one more separation from his family, but his wife Dorothy knew there was no way she could deter him from going even if she fully wished to do so, which she did not. She consciously acquiesced in the supportive role for her husband; what furthered his career and hence made him happy was something she wished almost as much as he. Their father's absence was not so keenly felt by Danice and Danny Jr. (Daniel James III), both in college, though it probably affected the youngest child, Claude (or Spud), who was still in high school.

6. Vietnam

President Lyndon B. Johnson and Secretary of Defense Robert S. McNamara decided to initiate aerial warfare against North Vietnam in March 1965 to reduce the flow of military supplies and troops from North Vietnam into South Vietnam and to make clear to the North that they would pay a heavy price for their continued support for aggression against the South. While the earliest American strikes against North Vietnam in operation "Rolling Thunder" encountered little opposition from a rudimentary antiaircraft system and no enemy aircraft, this situation changed rapidly by the end of March when North Vietnamese air defenses improved with effective radar-controlled guns. In July 1965 the North Vietnamese added to their defense the deadly Soviet built SA-2 surface-to-air missile (SAM), which destroyed several American aircraft within its first month of operation. The surface-to-air missile often forced American pilots either to jettison their ordnance to avoid being hit or to fly at lower altitudes, increasing their vulnerability to other types of antiaircraft weaponry. With gradual augmentation, the North Vietnamese proceeded by 1966 to develop the most dense and sophisticated ground defenses ever encountered by American pilots. These defenses were further strengthened after September 1966, when MIG pilots, using ground and air radar, became sufficiently numerous and well-trained to harass American pilots with hit-and-run tactics.

Political decisions also contributed significantly to the dangers and resulting casualties sustained by American fliers in their steady bombing operations. Fear of Chinese intervention dictated that American strategists refrain from all-out bombing of North Vietnam's industrial and shipping complexes, just as it obliged them to issue strict and unfavorable rules of engagement governing American planes in aerial combat. American fliers were forbidden, for example, to attack MIGs unless they first attacked American formations. This rule allowed the MIGs to intercept them under more advantageous terms, while it also prompted American planes to jettison ordnance prematurely in anticipation of being attacked. Even more disadvantageous, American planes were forbidden to attack MIGs on North Vietnamese airfields.[1]

Despite these difficulties, the Eighth Tactical Fighter Wing (Wolf Pack), commanded by Colonel Robin Olds, was able to claim an enviable battle record, shooting down twenty-four MIGs while losing only twelve planes to ground fire during a 180-day period in 1966.[2] The success of the Eighth was a tribute not only to the quality of the fliers selected by Olds to accompany him but also to the character and instincts of the leadership of the fighter wing.

Wing Commander Colonel Robin Olds and Colonel Daniel James, Jr., Olds's deputy commander of operations and after 1966 his chief assistant as vice wing commander, contributed significantly to the positive morale and successes of the Eighth Fighter Wing. Olds and James complemented one another's skills; the fliers called them Blackman and Robin, an obvious play on the dynamic duo of contemporary television, Batman and Robin, but the good-natured analogy caught the essential teamwork that existed between them.

Robin Olds was temperamentally suited to the role of fighter pilot–combat leader. The fact that he was raised in the military service aristocracy, his father a distinguished general, may have helped him in perfecting his tough and competent style. Forty-four years of age in 1966, he was a robust and athletic 6'3" tall and sported a flaring mustache, one that nearly half the fliers in the Eighth promptly imitated. He was respected because he had been battle-tested, a hero in World

War II, and because he demonstrated his skills in combat day after day. Olds was a natural leader who had a consuming desire to win and who tolerated nothing less in his subordinates. "If the meek are going to inherit the earth," he asked his fliers, "who the hell is going to give it to them?" This spirit is exemplified by his response one morning when the wing was getting ready for a good-sized mission on a heavily defended target. A weatherman interrupted the briefing with a report that bad atmospheric conditions would rule out the flight, causing one officer in the back, who was much relieved, to let out an audible "whew." Olds stopped his presentation, asked that officer to raise his hand, and calmly declared, "I want that son of a bitch off this base by nightfall."[3]

Olds was the first American flier in Vietnam to shoot down four MIGs and to claim a fifth, which would have made him the first U.S. ace in Vietnam, but the kill could not be fully certified. He often displayed reckless courage, especially when he was separated from his flight and felt less responsibility for the safety of his fellow pilots. One day he directed an assault of eight F-4s against twelve MIG-17s, lighter and more maneuverable planes than the F-4s. The MIGs employed the Lufberry circle defensive tactic. They preserved a tight turning circle with two, three, and four planes making separate orbits, thus providing coverage for each pilot's "six o'clock," the planes' most vulnerable position. The American planes attempted to break loose individual MIGs from their circles as the planes sped around one another at vicious speeds, with as much danger from collison as from guns. Olds downed one MIG and then found his fuel running low as the MIGs huddled for protection in their defensive wheel. Despite his vulnerability, Olds dove into a circle of MIGs. He later recorded the final moments of the engagement:

> "As I left the area by myself, I saw that lone MIG still circling and so I ran out about ten miles and said that even if I ran out of fuel, he is going to know he

was in a fight. I got down on the deck, about 50 feet, and headed right for him. I don't think he saw me for quite a while. But when he did, he went mad, twisting, turning, dodging and trying to get away. I kept my speed down so I wouldn't overrun him and I stayed behind him. He headed up a narrow little valley to a low ridge of hills. I knew he was either going to hit that ridge up ahead or pop over the ridge to save himself. The minute he popped over I was going to get him with a Sidewinder . . . I fired from about 25 to 50 feet off the grass and he was clear of the ridge by only another 50 to 100 feet when the Sidewinder caught him . . . I was quite out of fuel and all out of missiles and pretty deep in enemy territory all by myself, so it was high time to leave."[4]

Robin Olds chose Chappie James as his director of operations and later as his assistant as vice wing commander because he needed Colonel James's skills in motivating and managing the troops. He also needed an assistant who could handle effectively the myriad paperwork, personnel problems, and details of living that necessarily attended the encampment of 4,000 American servicemen in a foreign enclave at time of war.[5] Olds would have spent twenty-four hours a day in the cockpit if he had his way, but he understood as a modern commander that his unit's fighting efficiency depended on good ground support and, therefore, Chappie's style of leadership. Hence the two admired and respected one another, with James's regard for Olds especially strong.[6] Chappie came from a humble family. Robin's distinguished family, his successes at West Point in athletics and as an ace in World War II, and his marriage to a movie star impressed James as they did others. For James, Robin Olds was also the epitome of the fearless leader he had aspired to be when he decided to leave the sheltered life of school and home—close to his mother—to become a male champion.

Chappie worked tirelessly and enthusiastically to make

Ubon a good place for fliers to live and work and to perform the administrative functions of the wing, thereby releasing Olds for combat operations. He did so with his characteristic drive for excellence, but in that effort Chappie inevitably created problems for himself in the combat situation in Vietnam. Colonel James relished the daring slogan he used with the troops, which he later inscribed on his desk when he worked for the Department of Defense at the Pentagon: "Yea, though I fly through the valley of death, I shall fear no evil. For I am the 'meanest muthah' in the valley."[7] Yet his desk jobs since Bentwaters had deprived him of flying time and he was short in current tactical skills. Besides, the fighter aircraft was becoming increasingly complicated and required more flight time for mastery. Quick response in the cockpit was the key to remaining alive in combat, the F-4 having so many systems that it would be foolhardy to take one in combat without regular, even daily, flying. The switches were at the flier's fingertips, but in the stress of combat they had to be moved without looking. For pilots who flew the dangerous missions, everything was "touch and feel"; they focused prime attention on MIGs and SAMs and their wingman. James might have taken solace from the fact that his predecessor as vice wing commander of the Eighth, Colonel Vermont Garrison, a combat ace in both World War II and Korea (credited with shooting down five or more enemy planes), felt obliged to fly the F-4 in Vietnam with an instructor pilot in the back seat because he recognized that he could not, with his desk assignments, maintain his proficiency. While in Vietnam, Colonel James was averaging only six or seven sorties a month though the air force then held that eighteen to twenty sorties were necessary to maintain skill in the aircraft. Besides, he would be forty-seven years old shortly after he left Vietnam, while the average age of a front-seat pilot there was middle thirties. In addition, there was some question about the accuracy of his eyes, one officer recalling that Chappie's right eye seemed to divert to the side.[8]

Chappie's pride and courage, in addition to his terrible fear

*Colonel Robin Olds, commanding officer of the American air base at
Ubon, Thailand, with his vice wing commander, Colonel James, 1967.
(Courtesy of U.S. Air Force)*

of failure and disapproval by persons important to him, did
not permit him to fly with an instructor pilot. When he
climbed into the cockpit and donned his flight helmet with
black panther insignia, his backseater was a navigator. Colonel James flew seventy-eight combat missions plus many
other "no-counters" in Laos where it was easy to be shot
down in the vicinity of the Ho Chi Minh Trail and where, in
fact, he came close to losing his life on one mission.[9] When
William Kirk and William McAdoo, his old associates from
Bentwaters and Davis-Monthan, came to Ubon, James felt it
incumbent to lead the flight and introduce them to combat.[10]
He also accepted night missions, something he didn't like,
and performed well as a number-two pilot, another younger
flier taking the lead.[11] But even so, he was afraid some of the
fliers would lose respect for him if he did not fly more. Only a
select friend or two from "the family" was privy to his dilem-

mas. Inside the trailer where he lived, he revealed his depression. "I know what some of them are saying," he admitted wearily. "They think Chappie James hasn't got guts. How can you be a leader out here and command respect without flying with them?" None of his friends could persuade Chappie to treat himself more kindly. Undoubtedly, these concerns prompted him to lead the second flight of airplanes, one behind Robin Olds, in what would be the biggest and most successful American aerial victory in Vietnam, the Bolo MIG strike, January 2, 1967.[12]

The intent of the Bolo mission was to destroy the effectiveness of North Vietnamese fighter planes.[13] Since September 1966, North Vietnam had flown MIGs regularly as a defense weapon against American planes. Until that time, the big threats to U.S. strike aircraft had come almost entirely from ground defenses. The greater deployment of MIGs began to compromise the effectiveness of the attacking American planes, which were sometimes forced to jettison their bombs before reaching target in order to assume defensive formations against the threatening MIGs. American pilots, determined to put their bombs on target, increasingly found themselves in jeopardy with the more maneuverable MIGs making passes at them. The MIGs were likely to become an even greater threat in the future because American planes were being outfitted with electromagnetic countermeasures, pods placed on the wings of the aircraft designed to jam radar and hence eliminate the threat of SAMs. With the pods counteracting SAMs, U.S. fighter-bombers could attack targets with impunity because they could deliver their ordnance above the altitude for effective antiaircraft fire, hence necessitating greater reliance on aircraft by the North Vietnamese. The Bolo mission was designed, therefore, to deal a crippling blow to the North Vietnamese air force before it became large enough to defend targets effectively. The simplest way to accomplish that objective would have been all-out bombing and strafing missions against four well-known North Vietnamese bases: Gia

Lam outside Hanoi; Phuc Yen and Kep, northeast of Hanoi; and Cat Bi, which was southeast of the capital. Because political restrictions prohibited direct attacks on North Vietnamese airfields and the destruction of their planes on the ground, Bolo's overall aim to impair the enemy's air force employed a number of strategic ruses to accomplish its objectives. Because North Vietnamese aircraft could not be attacked on the ground, nor in the air unless they were attacking American planes, the essence of Bolo was to lure the enemy's planes into combat, then to destroy them before they could reach sanctuary in China or on their own airfields. To accomplish this, those in charge of the mission set an elaborate trap for the North Vietnamese. American planes would cover the four main airfields simultaneously, two, Gia Lam and Phuc Yen, from Ubon in the west, and the other two, Kep and Cat Bi, from Da Nang in the east. Sixty birds would be committed, thirty-two from Ubon and twenty-eight from Da Nang, thus creating a pincer effect. No matter which way the North Vietnamese pilots turned, they would find a wall of American fighter planes.[14] Flight strategy called for several waves of flights of American fighters from both Ubon and Da Nang at five-minute intervals. Stringing out the attack force assured a longer period of coverage for each airfield and increased hazards for MIG challengers, which could be kept in the sky by continuous hassling until they ran short of fuel. American planes then would pounce on them in this weakened state before they landed.

The critical issue for the entire mission was, of course, to get the MIGs off the ground. Because the North Vietnamese were much quicker to attack F-105s than F-4s (because the F-105 was the less maneuverable of the two), the commands at Ubon and Da Nang took elaborate precautions to disguise their F-4s as F-105s. ECM (electronic countermeasure) pods were placed on the F-4s for the first time, in keeping with their usage on the F-105s. In addition, F-4 pilots used airspeeds, radio calls, and communications of the F-105s in order to resemble them on North Vietnamese radar.[15]

D-Day for Bolo was set for January 2, 1967. Departure was delayed for over an hour by bad weather reports, a solid undercast from ground level to altitudes of 7,000 feet; this meant the American planes would not be able to see and divert from SAMs, though the pods were designed to minimize this danger. More serious, MIGs that risked combat could escape into cloud cover and the plan to cap the airfield by preventing enemy planes from landing was jeopardized.[16]

The MIG pilots in the vicinity of the Phuc Yen airfield, which Olds's lead flight reached at three o'clock in the afternoon, were at first reluctant to give battle. Olds and the three other pilots on this flight made two passes over the field before they made contact. Then combat began in the Red River Valley, lasting about ten minutes all together, with the planes flashing at one another like lightning bolts in all directions. Despite the transparent visibility above the clouds, there was no time to count accurately the number of MIGs engaged. There was barely time to think; reactions in the cockpit became instinctive and instantaneous. It was the fastest men had ever flown against one another with so many planes engaged.

As Olds's flight made its third pass, it was joined by Colonel James's flight above and to the right of the former. At that point the MIGs began to pop through the clouds and to attack Olds and the planes with him. Coming from all positions and angles, they probably were astounded when they recognized they had unsuspectingly challenged F-4s. Colonel James's flight called out the locations of the first MIGs. One disappeared quickly into the clouds, but Olds managed to gain position on a second. As it turned, Olds maneuvered his plane above the MIG and held there upside down to await the MIG pilot's decision to turn. Olds then rolled down his back and released sidewinders for the first aerial victory of Bolo.[17]

Colonel James's flight, after sighting MIGs for Olds, was itself attacked by three MIGs, two from the front and one below at the "five o'clock" position. Chappie's backseat pilot, Lieutenant Robert Evans, saw the MIG-21 approaching the number three and number four planes in the flight from the rear and ordered them to take evasive action while Colonel James concentrated on the planes above him and to his left, though without consequences. Meanwhile the MIG from five o'clock was approaching James's plane. His wingman, Captain Everett T. Raspberry, called, "Ford Leader, MIG at five o'clock, break right." To have broken left would have exposed the F-4 to the vulnerability of being shot at from directly behind. Amid the chaos of those first seconds of contact with the MIGs, Colonel James and his backseat pilot might not have heard the communication. Raspberry called him again, this time, "Chappie, MIG at five o'clock, break right," but Colonel James's plane failed to take evasive action, perhaps because James continued to concentrate on the North Vietnamese planes approaching from head on. Captain Raspberry on Colonel James's left then turned to protect Chappie by putting his plane between his flight leader and the MIG on Chappie's right.[18] As the silver MIG with its red star sped by, Captain Raspberry executed a rolling maneuver and placed himself in perfect position at the MIG's six o'clock at a range of 3,500 feet. Raspberry later recalled, "I assume that the MIG pilot was not aware of my position. . . . I fired the sidewinder and observed the missile home up his tailpipe. As soon as the missile detonated, the MIG-21 tumbled and stalled out. The aircraft went into a slow spiral, falling toward the undercast." Colonel James, who observed Raspberry's attack, followed the MIG and witnessed as it burst into flames and disappeared into the clouds.[19] Seven MIG-21s were destroyed by the first three flights from Ubon, a significant percentage of North Vietnamese aircraft then available. The mission was an enormous source of confidence for American fighter pilots inasmuch as no American planes were lost.

That night at the officers' club, Wolf Pack fliers partied superbly. For a few brief minutes earlier in the afternoon, they had used the skills for which they had been training for years, and they had performed beyond reasonable expecta-

*Colonel Daniel James, Jr., stands in front of his F-4C Phantom at
Ubon, Thailand, where he commanded the second flight of
airplanes in the Bolo MIG air strike, January 2, 1967.
(Courtesy of U.S. Air Force)*

tions. Chappie bought "Ras" a couple of drinks and congratulated him on his accuracy against the MIG-21. The story
spreading around the club that Captain Raspberry had saved
Colonel James's life, by rolling in and getting the MIG while
Chappie flew number two on Raspberry's left, was accepted
"with friendly grins." The fliers were impressed by the fact
that Chappie had been in the Bolo mission to begin with,
something he easily could have passed up, and they were
"glad to get him back safely." Some would be critical later,
however, when James's unlimited need for achievements
would lead him to boast about the number of missions he flew
in Route Package 6 (the Hanoi-Haiphong area), when in fact

nearly all his missions were in the less dangerous, though still hazardous, areas in the lower section of North Vietnam.[20]

That the other fighter pilots at the club had no difficulty approving of Colonel James's role in Bolo reflected more than their admiration for his courage. They knew that he was an important contributor to the team in other ways as well. As always, he was an inspirational leader for the others and performed exceptionally as articulator for the command. One officer, an air traffic controller, recalled: "I always enjoyed the morning briefings because of his excellent command of the English language and his knack for making any subject interesting. If anyone could rally a group of conscientious objectors into battle . . . it would have been [Colonel] James."[21] James also contributed to morale by remaining a close friend of many fliers who had known him personally since their days together at RAF Bentwaters. James had a very large and enthusiastic following at Ubon. His ethic, "We work hard and we play hard," appealed to men who were confronted with daily emotional strain, and, as ever, he loved to sing fighter pilot songs at the bar and enjoyed the good-natured camaraderie of the fraternity after the workday was over. He was also instrumental in establishing the practice of having torchlight parades for fliers who had completed 100 missions or who had been recovered after being shot down. As deputy wing commander, Colonel James also performed the paper and personnel work for the wing. His most important functions involved planning flight missions and assuring that planes, weapons, and pilots were available to fulfill those missions. He also met with an unending flow of dignitaries, including congressmen, generals, and royalty who visited the base, when either he or Olds were obliged to receive them. For all these services and "his celerity and accuracy in judging fluctuating combat requirements while maintaining relations with the local people," Colonel James was awarded the Legion of Merit by the secretary of the air force.[22]

One of Colonel James's most important, though least tangible, contributions to morale at Ubon was his enthusiastic endorsement of U.S. presence in Vietnam, which helped to allay discouragement and resentment in the military over denunciations of the war by black leaders at home. When James heard, in the summer of 1967, that Stokely Carmichael had asserted that "Negroes were ready to fight in the United States for their rights, but not in Vietnam," Chappie was reported in the *New York Times* as asserting that "thousands of Negroes were fighting in Vietnam" and "when we go home we'll have to live down the trouble he [Carmichael] and other idiots like him have built."[23] James also took exception to the emphasis of black leaders on purely domestic goals; he believed that blacks would benefit more in the United States when they established their reliability at times of the country's wars and national emergencies. Colonel James declared to the *Times* reporter: "We must speak out firmly against them [extremists] and their violence." He assailed particularly the idea that black extremists had the right to speak for the majority of their race. "This thing got to me," he told the *Times,* "the lawlessness, rioting, men like Stokely Carmichael acting as if they speak for the Negro people." All of James's learning as a youth, as well as the insights from his own successful career, were invoked in his passionate response to Carmichael. He adhered to an ideal of the United States that transcended particularistic identification. For James, the blacks' "right to fight" in Vietnam was an important step toward their acceptance as Americans; the United States would reward all persons equitably as long as they accepted its premises and worked diligently and patriotically within the system. This was the reason, he told *New York Times* newsman Peter Braestrup, that he was "an American first, a black second."[24]

While in Vietnam, Colonel James attempted to offset what he judged to be the pernicious influence of black and white dissidents in the United States by writing an essay, later reprinted in *Stars and Stripes,* for the Freedom Foundation contest in 1967. That essay, "Freedom—My Heritage, My

Responsibility," merited this conservative organization's George Washington Medal that year. It read in part:

> The strength of the United States of America lies in its unity. It lies in free men blessed and ordained with the rights of freedom working to provide, build, enjoy and grow. Those who would subvert us—or any free people—try to disrupt this unity by breaking the small parts from the whole—driving in the wedges of fear and discontent.
>
> I am a Negro and therefore I am subject to their constant harangue. They say: "You James are a member of a minority—you are a black man." They say: "You should be disgusted with this American society—this so-called democracy." They say: "You can only progress so far in any field that you choose before somebody puts his foot on your neck for no other reason than you are black." They say: "You are a second-class citizen."
>
> My heritage of freedom provides my reply. To them I say: "I am a citizen of the United States of America. I am not a second-class citizen and no man here is unless he thinks like one, reasons like one or performs like one. This is my country and I believe in her, and I believe in her flag, and I'll defend her, and I'll fight for her and serve her. If she has any ills, I'll stand by her and hold her hand until in God's given time, through her wisdom and her consideration for the welfare of the entire nation, things are made right again."
>
> Today's world situation requires strong men to stand up and be counted—no matter what their personal grievances are. Our greatest weapon is one we have always possessed—our heritage of freedom, our unity as a nation.[25]

One tangible response to that essay may be indicative of its general effect on morale among the American military in

Vietnam and throughout the world. It came in the form of a congratulatory letter from a sergeant who earlier had served with James in Korea. After praising Colonel James for being "what the enlisted troops refer to as an enlisted man's officer (The last time I saw you face-to-face you were a Captain and everyone called you Chappie.)," he addressed James's patriotic comments. "You make very clear that you're proud of your race as well as mine or any race as long as it's the American race. And that is the reason for this letter Col. just to let you know that *all* of your troops are behind you."[26]

By the end of 1967, the command at Ubon had been replaced. Colonel Olds, to become Brigadier General Olds in June 1968, returned to the United States after more than 150 combat missions to become commandant of cadets at the U.S. Air Force Academy through January 1971.[27] He came home with a remarkable record, as deserving of consideration as hero as he was after World War II when those accolades were gratefully extended to him. But the climate of opinion at home had changed and Olds became impatient with the antiwar sentiment that had grown while he was in Southeast Asia and with the fact that his fellow officers were still being asked to risk their lives in Vietnam under disheartening rules of warfare. With four MIG kills in Vietnam, he was a likely speaker on circuit for the air force, but his strong feelings clashed with reporters and even with members of the Nixon administration. While Olds's speaking out against the conduct of the war in Vietnam was understandable, he, like General MacArthur in Korea, was suppressed, his hero status notwithstanding. Reputedly, President Nixon, while reading the sports pages of the *Washington Post,* came across Olds's remarks at a gridiron banquet that were critical of the country's half-hearted prosecution of the war. Thereafter, Olds lost favor with the administration; he retired as a brigadier general after serving in his last assignment as a safety officer at Norton Air Force Base.[28]

Colonel James, a subject of considerable interest in the Johnson administration since championing participation by blacks in the Vietnam War, was greeted by LBJ at the White

House and given a hero's welcome on December 13, 1967. He got the full Johnson treatment, the arm around the back, the knee-to-knee, steady-eyed talk, a hand-shaking session for photographers, and introduction to White House reporters and passers-by. Before the president finished, he remarked that Colonel James's presence was a testimonial to the "progress that the services have made advancing people on merit without regard to color." The colonel then echoed an administration line that U.S. air power was gradually reducing the ability of the North Vietnamese to fight. He also endorsed the bombing of Haiphong harbor, and, when asked about morale in his unit, responded with predictable histrionic flair, "My fighter pilots have always had great morale."[29] The following morning a genial picture of the meeting appeared on page six of the *Washington Post*. The two would later exchange letters. President Johnson, writing Colonel James of his pleasure in hearing that the colonel had referred to their previous meeting in a public address, added, "Whatever your platform—lectern or cockpit—it is a good day for the cause of peace and freedom when you are on the job." Colonel James replied, "To say that I was pleased to receive your letter is the understatement of the year. I have been privileged to give wide circulation to our beliefs and the confidence and respect we have for our Chief."[30]

Assignment to Eglin Air Force Base, fifty miles from Pensacola, gave Colonel James an opportunity to spend more time with his sister Lillie and brother Tony and, of course, to be close to his own wife and children. James was proud of his family and very fond of his children, but he was an intense, extremely busy man whose prime interest was his career. He invariably worked twelve-hour days when at home and was separated from his family for long periods by overseas duty and, later, by extended series of speaking engagements. His wife Dorothy confessed that she never could slow him down, as his life continuously assumed the form of a steady rush. Golfing was one of his few recreations, though even here he played in an intensely competitive manner. When James was

After returning from Vietnam Colonel James has conference with President Lyndon B. Johnson at White House, December 13, 1967. (Courtesy of U.S. Air Force)

serving at Eglin, his daughter Danice, a graduate of Florida A & M, was a stewardess for TWA and soon would marry an air force physician, Dr. Frank Berry. Danny James was completing studies at the University of Arizona and soon would become an air force aviator and later a combat pilot in Vietnam. The third James child, Claude (Spud) was still in high school.

Vietnam was a personal victory for Chappie James. He had acquired unusual status through his association with Robin Olds and the remarkable Eighth Tactical Fighter Wing at Ubon, and he would enjoy Olds's support for promotion to general. He also had broken from the pack of over 5,000 colonels by his winning the Freedom Foundation Medal and by his forthright denunciation of extremism at home. The summons to the White House was a clear signal that he was viewed as a political asset and that henceforth he would be given special consideration by the powers in Washington.

7. A Returning Warrior

Although Chappie James had served with distinction as vice wing commander of an outstanding fighter wing in Vietnam, he won no immediate promotion for his efforts. He was reassigned as number-two officer at Eglin Air Force Base in Florida. There were rumors that he was considered for assignment as wing commander at Myrtle Beach, South Carolina, but the idea was shelved when it met with disfavor by influential residents.[1] Being forced to remain in the same position was discouraging, all the more so because Chappie knew that no black air force officer in the integrated service ever had been assigned the top post on a base in the continental United States (General Benjamin O. Davis, Jr., commanded in the Philippines).[2] Colonel James may have confided to close friends that he believed racial discrimination was holding him back, but he avoided raising the issue publicly. His suspicions probably were accentuated by the fact that he was passed over in his bid for promotion to brigadier general in 1969.[3]

James had worked hard for that promotion, and he had powerful political allies working for him as well. Michigan Congressman Charles C. Diggs, Jr., his old friend from flight days at Tuskegee, had pressured key members of the House concerned with the military, L. Mendel Rivers and Robert Sikes, on Chappie's behalf.[4] Rivers chaired the House Armed Services Committee and Sikes, from James's home district in Florida, the Military Construction Subcommittee of House Appropriations; both were senior members, staunch supporters of the military, and very knowledgable in accomplishing their pet projects. Sikes advised Diggs that Colonel James was among only 300 who were receiving final consideration from a pool of 7,000 other colonels for the seventy-seven openings for general then available.

In addition to employing Diggs's good offices, Colonel James also contacted Rivers and Sikes personally and wrote them in an ingratiating manner. Witnessing Rivers making a request for appropriations on the Hill, James wrote him, "It is a source of comfort that I shall continually convey to the men in the field that we have great lawmakers like you who understand the need for the capability of our military element of national powers."[5]

Bob Sikes was especially fond of James, the two having met often in Sikes's office when the colonel was in Washington. Sikes professes that he personally looked into James's military record and deemed him worthy of promotion to general officer before he made a number of contacts in an effort to help James secure a promotion.[6]

Colonel James sought numerous opportunities thereafter to befriend both Rivers and Sikes. He wrote Sikes, who was preparing for reelection, that he "would continue to support" the congressman because of his vigorous support for the military and because of their personal friendship.[7] And when an American aircraft met with an unprovoked attack by North Koreans in early spring 1969, James wrote both Rivers and Sikes that he endorsed their view that the United States should react with force. "I believe," he wrote Rivers, "that we have spoken softly long enough. We have the big stick. I think it is high time we use it"; and to Sikes he wrote in sycophantic terms, "Thanks again for standing tall in a forest of midgets."[8]

Overtures of this type helped James to win powerful friends. Both men also recognized that Chappie could be a useful ally at a time when public reaction against Vietnam was adversely affecting support for the military. What made James attractive to persons like Rivers and Sikes was not only his combat record and image as a fighter pilot who was black, but also his sincerity and the fact that he was articulate enough to be persuasive. These reasons prompted Rivers to ask Chappie to speak on Vietnam and patriotic subjects in South Carolina, and Sikes did the same in his home district as well.[9]

James's relationship with Rivers and Sikes resembled his loyalty to his "family" in the air force. Long after he had achieved his promotion to general officer and after either of these men could shake the tree to produce military plums, Chappie still would be accounted their friend. He spent the day of L. Mendel Rivers's funeral with the Rivers family. Bob Sikes professes that Chappie was one of the few he could count on as a friend after Common Cause's allegations against him for improper gains and after he was relieved of his post on the House Appropriations Committee.[10]

Chappie James was widely acclaimed when he returned from Vietnam. Although that conflict produced no celebrated warriors, James probably approximated one for Americans who supported U.S. involvement there. While Robin Olds, despite his distinguished combat record, rapidly lost favor, Colonel James was in demand as a speaker. From April 1968 through March 1969, James delivered more than seventy talks to a variety of audiences, including service clubs, church organizations, and air force dinners at bases across the country.[11] He also spoke on three occasions to organizations in Congressman Sikes's hometown in Crestview, Florida. Another large part of the speaking itinerary was reserved for Boy Scouts of many cities and to high school assemblies and graduations. In addition, James was invited to address the Capitol Flying Club in Washington, D.C., attended by two hundred persons including numerous congressmen; the Fort Worth (Texas) Chamber of Commerce for an Armed Forces Day celebration; the IBM Management Conference in Omaha; and the National Insurance Agency Association in Atlantic City. He also participated in the Mike Douglas television program on May 30, 1968, and the Jim

Conway television program from Chicago, March 3, 1969. Colonel James received numerous civic honors plus state and even national awards during the same period. The city of Pensacola made March 14, 1968, an appreciation day in his honor, and in July Bridgeport, Connecticut, conferred on him the title of honorary parade marshal for its annual Barnum Day Festival celebrating Independence Day.[12] In June 1969 he won the first Outstanding American Award by the state convention of Florida Jaycees.[13]

Response from these basically conservative groups was positive, even enthusiastic. A Scout executive for the state of Florida wrote President Johnson after James addressed four hundred of his Explorer Scouts: "Colonel James articulated the need for us to man the ramparts of freedom as well as anyone I have heard. He chastized those who divide our nation by their demonstrations, their riots and their taking into their own hands the laws of our nation."[14] The president of Colorado State University, who attended Colonel James's address to an air force ROTC unit on his campus, wrote the commander of the Tactical Air Command with similar appreciation: "The only regret I have about this exercise is that Colonel James will not be making a similar appearance on every major college campus in the land. In making this statement I speak from thirty-five years experience on campuses."[15]

And from mothers and wives who watched him on television opposing Gary Merrill's antiwar position, one wrote Jim Conway, "[Colonel James's] dignity in combating the tirade by Gary Merrill was wonderful to see. I wish that young people all over this country would be able to hear such a man speak, with his authority."[16] Another wrote the host of the same show: "It was a very rewarding exchange because it came when my two sons (12 and 14) were home for lunch. With two of their brothers in service now, they need this reassurance [from Colonel James]. Try to have him back."[17]

A chamber of commerce president responded to Colonel James's presentation with:

> We have enjoyed many guest speakers over the
> past months, all of which presented polished and
> well-organized speeches; however, I remember none
> who inspired our group as you have. It's a pleasure
> to hear a man who can talk about his love for our
> flag and nation without embarrassment. I wish that
> your ideals would receive as much national attention
> as the present protests that seem to dominate the
> news media.[18]

James's popularity, stemming from his meeting with LBJ,
his speeches across the country, and the invariable good
press that accompanied them, prompted one high school
teacher to write:

> We would like for you to send an autographed
> picture of yourself and any other material dealing
> with the Negro's role in Vietnam. We would also like
> for you to write an open letter to our student body as
> to the role they can play in the world community or
> on any subject you may like to discuss. We hope this
> will not be an imposition on your limited time, but
> any reply from you would be a source of inspiration
> to our youth as your fame and image has been a
> source of inspiration to all America.[19]

Colonel James's welcome reception was not difficult to
explain. His war record and personal values inspired confidence among whites because he was delivering an inspirational message not only about Vietnam but the future of the
country at a time when it seemed to be factionalizing. While
a majority of American whites were now mindful of the inequities experienced by blacks, they were not gladly disposed
to support blacks who were angry, law breaking, and un-
patriotic. Colonel James's record and speeches epitomized
hopes of many whites for blacks—that they would embrace
values of patriotism, responsibility for the society, and
achievement. He also helped restore the confidence of

whites that the United States was a great country and that it could be even greater when it more nearly practiced its principles of individualism free from prejudice. As his mother had prophesied, white Americans were willing to support qualified blacks who were responsive to the society's predominant values. While James's message pleased most white Americans, it was of course also intended for the interests of black Americans. His criticisms of rioting, lawlessness, and antiwar attitudes by blacks were prompted primarily by realization that these tactics ultimately would produce backlash and set back the cause of civil rights in the United States.

Colonel James broke down and wept on the day that Martin Luther King, Jr., was assassinated (April 4, 1968).[20] He was able to pull himself together on the following day, however, to make a previously scheduled presentation to air force officers on racial problems in the air force. An old Tuskegee friend was there and he described the atmosphere in that hotel as "very tense" as Colonel James got up to deliver his speech.[21] But James, in words almost identical with other talks, spoke with his customary faith in excellence, the system, and the future. William A. Coughlin, who attended that session, described it as follows in an article in the *Los Angeles Times*.

I remember Atlanta the morning after Dr. Martin Luther King was assassinated, when cities were burning across the nation. Colonel James was there to address an annual convention of the Air Force Association. I particularly remember one part of his speech:

"They say, 'You should be disgusted with this American society—this so-called democracy. You are black and here somebody is always going to remind you of that. You can only progress so far in any field that you choose before somebody puts his feet on your neck for no other reason than that you are a second-class citizen and you should be disgusted with the treatment you get here.'

"I say, hell, I'm not disgusted—I'm a citizen of the United States of America and I'm no second-class citizen either and no man here is, unless he thinks like one and reasons like one and performs like one. This is my country and I believe in her and I believe in her flag and I'll defend her and I'll fight for her and I'll serve her and I'll contribute to her welfare whenever and however I can.

"If she has any ills, I'll stand by her until in God's given time, through her wisdom and her consideration for the welfare of the entire nation, she will put them right."

Quite a speech for a black man in Atlanta on the day they were bringing Dr. King's shattered body home. It did not go unreported locally and it may have been more than coincidence that there were no riots in Atlanta on that weekend when they blazed so fiercely elsewhere.[22]

James's personal life was not free from embarrassments over race even as he was receiving adulation from the white community as did few contemporary blacks. Gas station attendants in the Deep South sometimes addressed him as "boy" despite the fact that he was dressed as a full colonel. James hardly ever wore civilian clothes in public—to minimize incidents like this.[23]

On one occasion a young woman pulled up in front of him at a service station in Fort Walton Beach, Florida, and declared, "I am late for my appointment with my hair dresser and besides, nigger, I don't have to explain all this to you!" At another time, at Otis Air Force Base in Massachusetts he overheard a security policeman call him a "goddamn nigger."[24] But Chappie managed to remain confident that progress would occur in race relations in his country despite incidents like the tragedy that befell Dr. King. The times were changing, especially among younger Americans. Furthermore, Chappie retained the faith of his childhood: equal opportunity and social equality for blacks would come once they applied themselves and a sufficient number of blacks attained excellence.

Colonel James worked diligently at Eglin Air Force Base and remained positive despite disappointments over his assignment there and evidence of increasing racial unrest in the nation. He often spent twelve- and fourteen-hour workdays but also found time for beer formations with the "young tigers" on Friday afternoons and numerous deep-dish olive pies now made entirely with Tangueray. (Chappie drank straight gin martinis, rejecting vermouth because, he said facetiously, "vermouth was the ingredient that caused drinkers to become sick.") He lost none of his skillful human touch either. He was "a hero" to his secretary, Julie McCaulay, who described herself as "true southern" at the time. Julie had been apprehensive about whether she could adjust to working for the black colonel, but she quickly came to admire "his sensitivity and thoughtfulness." He never asked her to pour coffee or to straighten up his desk; he remembered her with flowers on special days; and his telephone call on Christmas Day was from his whole family to her whole family. She also enjoyed his humor, such as when he referred to himself as "colorful," or when he got down on the floor and rolled in agony when he learned she was going on vacation, or when he instructed her to tell one of the numerous women attracted by his speeches that he had become KIA (killed in action). She was particularly impressed by his interest in the well-being of enlisted men. For Julie, he was a healer and a reconciler of persons—his humor, warmth, and consideration made people around him feel like family.[25]

Colonel James learned in March 1969 that he would be appointed to command Wheelus Air Force Base in Libya, the U.S. all-weather base where fighter pilots from Europe periodically were rotated for gunnery and bombing practice. He wrote a friend on March 10, "I am looking forward with much anticipation to having my own Wing at last. After being

Number Two so long, it is a challenge I will eagerly accept."[26] James was to report in July and assume command in October of that year. Robert C. Seamans, Jr., then secretary of the air force, looked upon Wheelus as a "key assignment" because the base was so important to the combat readiness of NATO defenses. He was told at the time that Chappie had "unique leadership qualities which had become evident as early as WWII." Seamans recalled that he was testifying before the Armed Services Committee, then chaired by L. Mendel Rivers, soon after Colonel James had been assigned to Wheelus. When Rivers asked the name of the new commander there, Seamans replied with some trepidation, "Colonel James," apparently concerned that the South Carolina congressman might disapprove on racial grounds. The air force secretary later reported, "Much to my amazement Mendel Rivers then delivered a very laudatory speech about "Chappie," noting that he was black and that he had been invited to South Carolina to speak before civic groups and had always received a standing ovation for his efforts."[27]

Colonel James's command in Libya would be greatly abbreviated by nationalistic and Pan-Islamic pressures, spearheaded by another colonel, the Libyan Khadafy.

8. Colonel James and Colonel Khadafy

In a predawn coup on September 1, 1969, Libyan Army units headed by a handsome young officer, Colonel Muammar Khadafy, seized key army posts and communication centers and announced the overthrow of Libya's King Idris. The revolt, which occurred only days before Colonel James was to assume command at Wheelus, had major implications for the United States. Khadafy's forces were nationalist fire-brands who viewed Wheelus, the only American air base in North Africa, as a remnant of Western imperialism and a contemptible insult to Libya's national independence. The ensuing pressure that Khadafy placed on the American government to close out Wheelus and retire its forces from Libya led to striking confrontations between the two colonels. James's responsibility to dismantle the American holdings at Wheelus, once the United States decided to pull out, was performed with such skill that he was able to enhance his favor in Washington and improve prospects for his promotion.

The United States had signed a Base Rights Agreement with Libya's monarchy in 1954 that guaranteed use of the air base, port facilities at Tripoli, and gunnery ranges until December 1970, for a sum of forty million dollars. Thereafter, either country could give notice of termination, with the agreement terminated one year after such notice or at minimum, therefore, in December 1971. The treaty with the

United States had been under criticism in Libya for some time before Khadafy's move. As early as March 1964 the Libyan Chamber of Deputies, in response to rising Arab nationalism, had resolved that negotiations should be initiated to terminate foreign bases. Although King Idris had continued to give reassurance to the American government about Wheelus, it remained thereafter hostage to turbulent politics. When Israel invaded Egypt and Syria in June 1967, mobs attempted to march on Wheelus, prompting the base commander to order fighter planes from Europe to return there while crews of planes permanently based at Wheelus were alerted to scramble and 6,300 American dependents were evacuated to Europe.[1]

Tensions subsided and the dependents returned, but Libyan hostility toward the American presence escalated again with augmenting oil prices, which made Libya increasingly independent of American military aid. American strategy to remain at Wheelus was aimed at mollifying nationalist critics by showing the utility of the base for Libya's defense and modernization. Americans would train the Libyan Air Force in the United States and at Wheelus and train Libyans employed at Wheelus in the use of automatic data processing and communications. The United States also would avoid offense to Libyan nationalism by minimizing contacts between American personnel and the native population: the air force would provide ample base facilities for personnel and would fly planes out of sight of the native population until they reached deserted stretches of sand that would serve as avenues to American gunnery ranges.

In the immediate aftermath of the Khadafy coup on September 2, 1969, Libyans placed the base under curfew at night, denied access to off-base air force and American civilian personnel, and cut off communications between the base and the American embassy in Tripoli. In response, the base commander who preceded Colonel James ordered the arming of his F-100s. He also strung wire at the gates and placed dumpsters and waste vehicles behind the wire while sentry dogs and trainees were posted close by. Colonel James assumed command on September 22 at a very tense time. The army officer's coup had succeeded and Colonel Khadafy's unstable genius predominated in the new regime. Khadafy already had demanded that the American government ground all aircraft at Wheelus and close the port that supplied most of the food and supplies for the base, in effect a demand that the base become immobilized.

Tensions between the two colonels, each with strong nationalistic feelings and each possessed of a sense of historic destiny, worsened when Khadafy's entourage held James accountable for either complicity or neglect in the so-called Jew in the box incident.[2] Daniel A. DeCarlo, a principal in the school system for dependents at Wheelus, had requested of James permission to repair band instruments abroad and had been denied. Regardless, he used the "tuba box" for his real purpose—to provide secret transportation for a Libyan Jew who feared for his safety under the revolutionary government. DeCarlo's friend was crated and loaded on a plane on September 23. James later recalled that when the plane landed at Malta, DeCarlo became concerned whether his friend was getting enough air. He asked the Maltese inspection guards to take a walk down the road and proceeded to open slightly the tuba box with a crowbar. The guards were suspicious and remained within view as DeCarlo opened the box. When they began to return to the plane, the professor, recognizing his ruse had been uncovered, opened the box to allow its occupant to escape. The Libyan Jew ran into the woods with a suitcase in each hand but was taken into custody by immigration officials, while the professor was apprehended, crowbar in hand.

The revolutionary government was incensed over the incident, claiming that it illustrated that the base perpetuated colonialism in Libya and raised suspicions whether the United States government, through Wheelus, might offer assistance and sanctuary to Libya's enemies. Khadafy's spokesmen immediately insisted on the right of inspection by

Libyans of all persons, goods, and cargoes leaving Wheelus, and an arrangement was reached permitting joint inspection between officials of both countries.[3] The Libyans then demanded the right to inspect incoming mail and to post guards at the gates of Wheelus, conditions Colonel James vigorously had opposed. But Ambassador Joseph Palmer, who was in charge of top-level negotiations with the new government, agreed in an effort to initiate amicable talks on the future of the base and American oil holdings in Libya.

The air force called for a firmer stance against Khadafy than did Ambassador Palmer: the United States should insist on its full rights under the agreement with the government of King Idris and should not prematurely withdraw its base at Wheelus before the expiration of that agreement. The commander of the Sixteenth Air Force, whose authority encompassed Wheelus, also advised his superiors that the American position in negotiations should be "to hold on to the base for the duration of the agreement." The United States might stress its utility to the Libyan Air Force and renegotiate an agreement or perhaps exploit the uncertainty of the new regime by buying time and hoping that it would be replaced before December 1971 by more realistic leaders.[4] The air force command believed Wheelus in American hands was important for NATO because American fighter wings got most of their weapons training there because of Libya's good weather. The wings were brought in from Europe, especially in the winter months, on a rotational basis, most fighter pilots spending two weeks every three months on the gunnery ranges. Because there was no comparable U.S. base, the air force stressed in its communications with the secretary of defense its "urgent need" to retain Wheelus.

Colonel James's role was critical in these complex dealings between the American and Libyan governments and in underscoring the air force's commitment to remain at Wheelus. Notes scribbled by General Eugene Le Bailley, commander of the Sixteenth Air Force, show that James helped formulate

the air force's position on Wheelus. The notes read in hand-
script: "James—can't get out of here. Libyans can't handle
[base] without trained people. . . . R.C.C. [abbreviation for
Khadafy's Revolutionary Command Council] making many
mistakes, if we can buy a year's time it's worth it. Must be
firm in Washington."[5] James also adopted a tough stance,
within his prerogatives under the Base Rights Agreement, in
his dealings with the Libyans. Flying had been closed down
at Wheelus since the coup, and Colonel James wanted training to resume for the F-100s permanently based there, a
muscle-flexing exercise.

A Libyan authority cautioned James that he first should
obtain approval of the RCC; James replied that he was following the Base Rights Agreement and was unwilling to seek
anyone's permission. Congressman Robert Sikes, who com-
municated with Colonel James by transatlantic telephone at
that time, remembers, "Chappie knew America needed that
base very much and if [Khadafy's] crowd took over it would
be the beginning of the end. He wanted the American embassy to take a much stronger stand than it did. Had Chappie's advice been followed, I am confident we would still have
Wheelus."[6] When, however, Colonel James reported the Libyan colonel's anxiety to the American embassy, Palmer advised him to delay flying the F-100s until ambassadorial talks
commenced with Libya's foreign minister.

In the interim, on October 18, there was a major incident at
Wheelus's main gate between Libyan troops and American
guards. Chappie rushed to the gate and stood there uncompromisingly to calm the fracas. He later recalled:

> "One day Khadafy ran a column of halftracks
> through my base—right through the housing area at
> full speed. I shut the barrier down at the gate and
> met Khadafy a few yards outside it.
>   He had a fancy gun and holster and kept his hand
> on it. I had my .45 in my belt. I told him to move his

hand away. If he had pulled that gun, he never would have cleared his holster. They never sent any more halftracks."[7]

On October 25, Ambassador Palmer, under instructions from the State Department, concurred with James's insistence on resuming military flights, and on October 29 two F-100s took off for a test flight. Thereafter, four U.S. military aircraft flew from Wheelus per day, routed over the water. Libyan authorities questioned the flights, but James declared his intention to continue and Khadafy finally agreed to authorize them.[8]

Finally, however, after more than a month of almost continuous pressure from Khadafy, the American government, despite opposition from the air force and Colonel James's protests, decided to withdraw from Wheelus; Americans would depart more than seventeen months before the expiration of their lease under the rights agreement. The United States did so because it feared Wheelus's future was ultimately nonnegotiable with the revolutionary government. Early evacuation at least might incur favor with the new rulers and forestall nationalization of American oil interests, a paramount consideration for American policy makers.[9] Ambassador Palmer first learned of Khadafy's intransigence over Wheelus when the two leaders met in Tripoli on November 19 amid angry crowd demonstrations against the United States. Palmer had sought Khadafy's approval for the resumption of training on the gunnery ranges at Wheelus but Khadafy had replied that all foreign troops would have to leave so that the Libyan people could achieve their freedom. Khadafy also used the meeting as a forum to denounce the United States for using Wheelus as a "base for aggression under NATO" and to condemn American involvement in Vietnam. Because Palmer believed that Americans would be forced out regardless, he reasoned that the Libyans should be given a "realistic early date" for withdrawal; hence he asked the State Department for authorization to offer return of the facilities by September 30. The agreement signed by both parties called for evacuation no later than June 30, 1970.[10]

What remained for the command at Wheelus was to remove or sell to the Libyans the base's demountable equipment while avoiding hostile confrontations until the base closed.[11] Colonel James was in charge of the American group that negotiated the disposal of property and there were many stormy sessions with his Libyan counterparts. It soon became apparent that each side had different perceptions of what base evacuation entailed. For the Libyans it meant little if any equipment was to be removed; at issue were such items as radar and other navigational equipment, generators, and hospital equipment. The American position was to sell only the property the United States could not use elsewhere. Colonel James assured the Libyan negotiators, however, that equipment needed by the air force and by the Libyans would be retained as long as possible, to enable Libya to secure replacements, and that American personnel would provide maximum assistance in training Libyans to use that equipment. These overtures were insufficient; the Libyans became truculent when it became apparent that the United States would take much of their removable property with them. On the issue of generators, James declared he would relay the Libyans' request that the generators remain at Wheelus but warned he would move them on his own initiative in the absence of approval from the air force. The Libyans were even more insistent and bellicose about retention of base radar. Congressman Bill Nichols of the Committee on Armed Services visited Wheelus during these negotiations and spoke with James. The congressman recalls:

> Colonel James explained to the [Khadafy] Government that the United States needed this radar system at one of our air bases at Zaragoza, Spain, but they still insisted that it be left. He told us that the day

prior to our arrival a group of young colonels had driven to the entrance gate at Wheelus demanding to see Colonel James again about the radar and that he had invited them to come on post and discuss the matter in his home. He told us that he invited the group into his house: that they sat in the very living room we were sitting in and that their driver came in with a submachine gun which he nestled in his lap as the conversation began. I asked Colonel James, "What did you do?", to which he replied, "I told the senior officer in charge that I was going to count to three and if that s.o.b. was not out of my living room by that time then I would physically throw him out." I asked the Colonel if the man removed himself, to which he replied, "Yes, and he was pretty quick about it." I can certainly understand why, because Chappie James was a magnificent physical specimen standing some 6'4" tall and was extremely impressive as an officer. [12]

Secretary of Defense Melvin Laird remained in close contact with James during this stage of negotiations. He made it clear that he wanted the equipment important to the United States to be moved out of Wheelus as quickly as possible, especially in light of ugly incidents surrounding the recent discussions. In consequence large cargo planes were moved into Wheelus at night and the valuable material was flown to other American bases, also at night. The Libyans were exasperated, but Colonel James performed his assignment well and thereby gained considerable recognition from the secretary of defense at the very time decisions were being made to add new general officers to the military for 1970. [13]

American operations at Wheelus wound down on schedule. Directives for evacuation were issued, travel by dependents halted, and the last American fighter planes on base were removed to England. On January 15, 1970, the transfer of facilities to the Libyans began, a process that was com-

pleted on June 11, 1970.[14] Colonel James gave a stirring
speech to those last fighter pilots before they took off on a
bright Mediterranean morning just as sunlight encircled the
base. His speech was recorded in the base newspaper at
Wheelus.

> Did you ever stop to think of the guys who flew
> out of here—aces like Jabara, Everest, Olds and
> Garrison—guys like Robbie Risner and Swede Lar-
> son, who are in the Hanoi Hilton now but who honed
> their tiger teeth many times over the sands of El
> Uotia [weapons range].
> Well, the hell with it! This isn't the end of it all.
> Just the beginning of a new chapter. Streaking
> through some other sky, some other time, to do what
> we have to do to maintain the professionalism
> required of our business.
> It's the beginning of a new era, a new place to do
> our thing that might be a little more difficult than El
> Uotia was. The real estate will probably be more
> limited, the run-in lines will probably be harder to
> see, the safety section of the briefing will be longer
> and more detailed because the error potential will be
> substantially increased.
> This is when the over-worked word "professional"
> that precedes the term "fighter pilot" gains true
> meaning. Those of us who answer the challenge
> prove that it does have meaning in the way we meet
> it.
> In other skies, on smaller ranges, fighter jockeys
> of the Air Force will still hone their teeth and stand
> ready at any time to meet the requirements as air
> policemen for the greatest power on earth.[15]

Colonel James was relieved of his command on March 25,
1970. He had been nominated for promotion to general by
President Nixon and that nomination had been approved by

the Senate and would take effect in July 1970. He also had been assigned, on the request of the secretary of defense, Melvin Laird, and his assistant secretary of defense for public affairs, Dan Henkin, to work at the Pentagon as assistant deputy to Henkin. James would be third man in that office behind Henkin and Dick Capen.

Chappie's new assignment reflected Laird's confidence in him, based on his impressive record in Libya, but it was also a tribute to the shrewd perception by Laird and Henkin that James had impressive credentials to influence public opinion positively on behalf of the military; the oversized and articulate black general with five rows of ribbons was bound to disarm foes of the Pentagon. The Defense Department would now be certain to get its side across, even to confirmed critics.[16]

Secretary Laird's determination to assign James to public affairs at the Pentagon helped influence the decision of an air force promotion board to recommend Chappie for general and the favorable review of that recommendation, which led to confirmation by President Nixon and Congress.[17] A military man holding a position in public affairs probably required a general's rank because he served as an intermediary between the armed services, the Defense Department, and the news media and public groups. For Laird, James's fitness reports, "leadership and operational skills," and success at Wheelus clinched the promotion.[18] The fact that James was also black was a consideration in his favor, though thirty other black colonels were denied promotion in the same selection process.

From James's four black contemporaries with whom he might be genuinely compared—Hannibal Cox, William Campbell, Charles Cooper, and Charles McGee, all colonels who had served many years as fighter pilots, though none were still in fighter pilot operations in 1970—there is strong praise for his selection. One stresses that Chappie deserved to be a general because "he was an excellent officer, a hard worker and solid performer and because he was the only black in the Air Force in a position where he could be visible." Another observes that while other senior black officers who were Tuskegee Airmen "*may* have deserved promotion, Chappie *surely* deserved promotion based on his ability and effectiveness." Colonel Charles E. McGee (ret.), a very successful fighter pilot in Korea who was promoted to major the same year as James (and promoted to colonel in 1969, five years after James), underlines the merit of James's selection, observing, "They couldn't have picked a better man." McGee stresses James's ability as a pilot, his leadership qualifications, and "his ability to deal with people at all levels." Only one has declared that anyone in the group would have been as deserving of promotion to general as James but that Chappie's flamboyance and eye-catching appeal together with Mel Laird's sponsorship were the keys to his success.[19] In addition, all the younger black fighter pilots—Clark Price, Thomas E. Clifford, William Earl Brown, Jr., and James "Tim" Boddie, Jr., then in middle ranks, later to be colonels or generals—unanimously endorse his promotion; they looked to James as their "pioneer" and "trailblazer."[20] Ultimately, Daniel James, Jr., became a general probably because the selection board decided that he was an outstanding military man with requisite skills who was also black. Incidentally, the fact that he finally received his college degree from Tuskegee Institute twenty-seven years after he had been expelled from that institution also helped in a small way to qualify him for the rank of general. He had taken many courses while in the service that Tuskegee could accept for credit; hence he became a general only one year after he was graduated from college.[21]

Daniel James, Jr., thus became the fourth black to hold the rank of general in the history of the armed forces and the second in the air force.[22] His predecessor in the air force, Benjamin O. Davis, Jr., a retired three-star general, had been appointed general in 1954, eighteen years after he was commissioned, while it took James twenty-seven years to become a general officer. Davis also bested James in years required to secure command of a wing—Davis became a wing commander seventeen years after his commissioning while James served twenty-six years before obtaining such a command.

The selection of James as general met with staunch approval from his many friends in the air force and the Congress, but it also produced charges from others that James was promoted merely for reasons of race. A group of disgruntled white colonels argued that Chappie would have remained a colonel were it not for the determination of the Department of Defense to put a new face on its higher officer corps. In effect, their position held that the military in its efforts to gain social acceptance was now lowering standards to reward blacks with top positions. When contacted by phone in Libya, Colonel James denied the implications that he was replacing General Davis as *the* black general in the air force; he remained faithful to his formula that ability and hard work produce success in the United States regardless of race or color. In explaining his promotion he said, "I was fortunate, but I feel like I worked for it and deserved it. I did a lot of driving and a lot of hard work and I had a lot of support from friends." He also attributed his own success to attending command schools, his Vietnam service, and his skillful work with the Libyan junta.[23]

From his friends, of course, no explanation was possible other than his competence. Congressman Sikes in a telegram wrote, "I know of no one more deserving of this recognition."[24] Major Denny Sharon, a close friend since Bentwaters, acknowledged warmly, "Dear Chief, or should I say General, Mag [Colonel Maglione] just called me with the great news. I can't tell you how happy I am for you. Guess this crazy promotion system has something in it after all. You've been a great credit to your country, Chappie. . . . You've had a tougher struggle than most but that will only make it taste so much sweeter."[25] Major Billy Patton, who flew at Davis-Monthan and at Ubon with Chappie, wrote, "Dear Chief, I knew it would happen and am so damn proud I could bust a button."[26] The president of Esso Standard in Libya congratulated Colonel James on his promotion and concluded, "Your assignment [in Libya] has not been an easy one, but the manner in which you conducted yourself has gained the admiration of the American community."[27] Dick Collins, another member of the Wolf Pack at Ubon, supported Chappie's selection, declaring, "One thing for sure; there ain't a guy in the Air Force who doesn't know you. . . . This reputation came mostly in the last couple of years and has been enhanced by your good work in Libya. Your value as an American is unparalleled in the Air Force."[28] From the Catholic chaplain at Ubon, the Reverend Tom Heffernan, came, "How truly happy I am for you. It couldn't happen to a nicer and better person."[29] An enlisted man from Bentwaters wrote his congratulations because "I have followed your career and admired you as a man and an officer."[30] And from Brigadier General Robin Olds came words that must have been appreciated. Olds wrote:

> Dear Chappie:
> No need to tell you how delighted I am with your nomination to Brigadier. And it goes without saying that the promotion selection was based on a record of accomplishments. . . . I am really happy for you and Dottie. It has been a long, hard pull for you both, with tears and heartaches along the way. The recognition is past due and richly deserved. All I can say is that I am proud, damned proud of you both.[31]

One of the most interesting congratulatory letters came from Chief of Staff, Supreme Headquarters Allied Powers, Europe, General H. M. Wade. Wade, an air force general who knew James well because Wheelus Air Force Base was part of his command, emphasized James's responsibility to comport himself in his private life in a manner worthy of the select group of general officers he would join. Wade seemed to be warning the newly nominated general that his "fighter jock" revelries now should be discreetly avoided. He declared:

> I am sure that you will realize, that is when you come down off cloud 9, that you now belong to a select group within the Air Force and the things that you do will be closely observed by all of those who serve with you. Some things will come easy and others will be harder, but you have my confidence and I know that you will do your utmost to uphold the high standards by which the Air Force operates.[32]

A *Washington Post* newswriter flew to Libya to interview the newly selected general in January 1970. He described James as the original Black Panther, noting the markings on Chappie's flight helmet, but he perceived that James saw himself as "a different breed of cat . . . [one who] fights for his country." The commentator observed that James preferred to think of his achievements as "an American success story."[33] Chappie's positive attitude would serve him well during his tenure as deputy and later as principal deputy to the assistant secretary for public affairs in the Defense Department during the critical period 1970 to 1974.

9. Into the Stars

By 1970, the lessons drawn by most liberal observers of the war in Vietnam were that intervention there had been a mistake and that the United States should withdraw: either Vietnam was not a strategic American interest or the gains for the United States in shoring up South Vietnam were disproportionately small when compared with the agonizing, divisive costs at home and the negative effects on domestic reform. Some in the American political center, more concerned about the effects of possible defeat in the loss of South Vietnam, might argue that Vietnam had been only a "great aberration" and that the United States could still save face in withdrawal by announcing "no more dominoes" but standing firm on the great balance of power issues in the future. Conservatives supporting U.S. presence in Vietnam argued the domino theory, but many also reasoned that withdrawal would have disastrous consequences for the future reliability of the United States in international relations. The stability of the international order and hence world peace depended on U.S. strength and the will to maintain and use that strength. To falter in Vietnam would cause nations that depended on the United States and those that feared the United States to suspect U.S. leadership. In this view, Vietnam was still a small cost compared with the dangerous consequences of withdrawal.[1]

It was this view that prevailed in the Nixon-Kissinger era of American diplomacy. Henry Kissinger described the dilemma of the Nixon administration in the late 1960s:

We could not simply walk away from an enterprise involving two administrations, five allied countries and thirty-one thousand dead as if we were switching a television channel. . . . As the leader of the democratic alliance we had to remember that scores of countries and millions of people relied for their security on our willingness to stand by allies, indeed in our confidence in ourselves.[2]

The reasons the Republican leadership chose to remain in Vietnam were small consolation to the increasingly large number of Americans who passionately opposed the war. When Nixon's determination that the United States not be reduced to a "pitiful helpless giant" led to bombing Cambodia and later sending American troops there in April 1970, antiwar sentiment escalated further. It was intensified by the tragic shooting of protesting students at Kent State University (May 14, 1970) and further disruptions at more than 400 universities. Under the circumstances, the Department of Defense, with its headquarters in the Pentagon, became a symbol of the unpopular war and the object of numerous demonstrations. Officials there, including Secretary of Defense Laird, believed that it was imperative that the Defense Department be able to convince the public of the administration's viewpoint or risk further deterioration of the American position on Vietnam. For these reasons, Laird made his first appointment every workday in the early 1970s with Dan Henkin, his assistant secretary of defense for public affairs.

During the period 1970 to 1974, when General James worked in public affairs, Secretary Laird and Assistant Secretary Henkin were particularly concerned with key issues affecting the public image of the Defense Department: the department's credibility with the Pentagon news corps; student opposition to the war in Vietnam and related military activities; racial unrest in the military; and the activities of POW-MIA wives, an organization of about a thousand wives, mostly of navy and air force officers who had been shot down and were either prisoners or missing in action in Vietnam. These women were deeply grieved over their husbands' plight, especially their bad treatment as prisoners, and over their own frustration in raising families as single parents year after year, some since 1966, while the war continued with seemingly no end in sight. They merited much public sympathy in the media and defense officials feared they easily could become still another focus of antiwar, even antimilitary, opinion.[3]

The Defense Department needed someone with General James's record, personality, and convictions to deal effectively with these problems. James had no sympathy for radical protesters, evidenced by his assertion: "And to those who say they'll change the government or burn it down, I say, 'like hell you will.' For they haven't reckoned with the millions of us who raised our right hand years ago and pledged with our lives to protect and defend this great nation from forces foreign and domestic." He was "an unabashed champion of the Nixon administration but no less a champion of Kennedy or Johnson," or, as he declared, "I'm for the president, no matter his name."[4] James's successes in the Pentagon were so dramatic that his boss, Assistant Secretary Jerry Freidheim, later remarked, "No general officer could have done the job as well as Chappie and many could not have done it at all."[5] These achievements accounted for James's rapid ascent into the stars, his acquiring two more during his four years in the Pentagon while establishing strong claims for a fourth star, the pinnacle of the peacetime military.

James's exuberant fighter-pilot style appealed to the Pentagon press corps. Reporters such as Fred Hoffman of the Associated Press, Lloyd Norman of *Newsweek,* and Bob Schieffer of CBS News warmed to Chappie's offhand manner and humor (one morning he wore the robes of his recently conferred honorary doctorate from the University of Akron to the press conference). As Schieffer recalls, "We reporters thought he was a great guy." Besides, they respected him as a hard worker who used his star to ferret out useful information from the Pentagon's labyrinths. Unquestionably, he enhanced the government's credibility with those who were responsible for relaying Pentagon news to the American public.[6]

Because Jerry Freidheim was more likely to handle news briefings in the first years of Chappie's tenure in the Defense Department, James was assigned primary responsibility for influencing student opinion in high schools and on college campuses. He looked upon this assignment as if he were engaged in a *kulturkampf* with the outcome determining the allegiance of the largest generation of youth in American history and hence the very survival of the nation.[7]

James appealed to high school graduates with his positive attitudes. "Call me idealist," he quipped, "but that's better than quitter, destroyer, or anarchist." He reminded students that he once had more reason to become embittered and drop out than most of them: "I was reminded at every turn that I was different because I was born that way and there were going to be different rules for me and the other guy all my life, but I had faith and a mother who told me, 'don't give up hope,' and 'take advantage of every opportunity that comes your way.'" James concluded with statements such as, "You can do more from the top with authority and knowledge than from the bottom, lighting a torch. Things are better now than they were ten years ago or five years ago. We in the Department of Defense have a slogan—a legacy from [coach] Vince Lombardi—'In this league we run forward for daylight, we don't dance around in the backfield.'" By the time he finished, the students were on their feet with an ovation, many remaining after his talk for autographs.[8] Occasionally, of course, he had to deal with hecklers or malcontents, but General James's dramatic routines were so ingenious that he could silence them by singing a spiritual, "Motherless Child" or "You Must Come in the Door," and then continuing with his presentation.[9]

On college campuses the battle was more complicated and

the outcome more uncertain. One of the first college appearances for James occurred on May 8, 1970, when he was
invited to participate in a ceremony dedicating an Air Force
Association at the University of Florida, Gainesville, and to
make several appearances before student and community
groups. During one of those meetings, General James was
asked a number of pointed questions about Vietnam; one
student, who was no longer able to contain disappointment
with his responses, finally asked "how a black man like yourself could support the intolerable racist war in Vietnam."
General James replied, "Look, friend, I have been black for
fifty years, which is more than you will ever be, and I know
what I believe in"; he went on to give plausible reasons for
American presence in Vietnam. Students applauded his presentation. General James's appearance was credited with de-
fusing the tense atmosphere on the Gainesville campus,
including a strike planned against the university the following week. A local physician who attended some of James's
speeches later wrote and congratulated him for his "remarkable service on behalf of national defense" because, he reminded, "the home front is a sector too, and in the present
circumstances a hell of a sector. Within the military hier-
archy there are too damn few operational officers [like your-
self] who are eloquently capable of presenting the feeling of
the man behind the gun."[10]

At the University of Pittsburgh's Stephen Foster auditorium James addressed students concerned about Vietnam. A crowd of students carrying peace signs jostled and
taunted him while he walked with a small entourage on his
way to the auditorium, where the mood of the students was
unfriendly, many standing on the sides rather than taking
seats. After General James began to speak an angry group
burst through the door carrying antimilitary slogans and
creating such commotion that he was forced to suspend his
presentation. The program would have ended had it not been
for the presence of the student in charge who went to the
microphone James was using, adjusted it downward to her

5'2" size, and declared, "Wait a minute! We asked him to talk to us. If you can't stand here and let him talk, then get out of here!" The more belligerent students walked out but most, chastened by one of their peers for their lack of courtesy, put their signs down and listened. James began again: "I won't always agree with you, but here are the facts. . . . Adequate defense is a strategy for peace. We can't afford to cave in in Vietnam because that will send a signal of American weakness to the communist world and will invite their aggression. . . . Nobody dislikes war more than warriors. . . . We are withdrawing from Vietnam under President Nixon at a rapid rate and will continue to do so. The president wishes to stop the war but he refuses to crawl to a peace table." James received a standing ovation.[11]

The University of Wisconsin at Madison was one of the citadels of the antiwar movement. Antiwar generational solidarity there had produced violent protest; militants had blown up a math building in the summer of 1970 because it allegedly trafficked in technology for war, and a researcher had been killed in the blast. Student leaders also had challenged Secretary of Defense Laird to debate the merits of the war and promised a large turnout if he would appear.[12] Although Laird was scheduled to speak at a Madison Inter-Service Club luncheon in the University of Wisconsin field house, he declined the invitation at the last minute and delegated the responsibility to James.

When the students learned of the substitution they decided to protest James's presence by scheduling a speech by Chicago Seven defendant Rennie Davis and Weatherman Linda Evans. Davis lauded the bombing of the university building, which had such appalling consequences, and predicted, "If the government doesn't stop the war we are going to stop the government."[13] He urged students to "shake down" faculty members for $100 or $150 to buy old cars that would break down in May demonstrations on the main thoroughfares in Washington leading to the Pentagon. After hearing Davis and Evans, more than 2,000 protesters marched to the field house to demonstrate against General James.[14]

The atmosphere within the field house was hardly sanguine for the speaker either. While the crowd outside shouted and gave coordinated chants, the university chancellor who introduced James called for "the most rapid withdrawal of our troops from Vietnam within the national interest." Meanwhile, student waiters and waitresses wore peace signs on their uniforms and slipped mimeographed peace messages into folded napkins for the 1,000 persons at the banquet.[15]

"I got the message," James said in a booming voice when he got up to speak. "We got the message a long time ago, but we ask for your tolerance as we search for an early solution. The Nixon administration would like to get all combat forces out of Vietnam. We have met or beat every commitment to withdraw forces we have made. But," he added, "the other side must also show good faith. We cannot, for example, compromise the welfare of our prisoners, nor forget them. Meanwhile, we do not help our bargaining position with North Vietnam by divisive and destructive actions at home." It was laudatory, he said, to speak of "freedom now, but unless the United States is a strong united nation, there will be no place to be free in." His speech was interrupted by applause many times and again he was given a standing ovation.[16]

University of Wisconsin blacks had boycotted the speech; they let General James know, however, that he could speak to them at the Afro-Center on campus. En route, James and his entourage were pelted by snowballs and their cars surrounded by angry, taunting students from the Davis-Evans conclave. At this juncture, General James decided to hail a cab to get to the student center in order to avoid further confrontations in his military vehicle.

Upon arrival at the Afro-Center, General James noted that a young white newsman and whites with a television crew had been denied entrance to the discussion. James was incensed that they were forced to stand outside in freezing weather. He chided the president of the Afro-Union that what he had just witnessed was the most flagrant case of racism he had seen on campus. General James then refused to enter the building unless whites also could enter; they were permitted to do so.[17]

General James's message was "you've got to work within the system; my way is slower, but it is surer. Use the advantages given you for an education and then serve the total community as well as the black community." When queried about blacks being cannon fodder in Vietnam, he explained that blacks didn't get the deferments whites did for schooling and occupations, hence their disproportionate number of casualties in Vietnam. He probably was surprised when another angry questioner asked what his position would be if the State Department ordered him to support the South African government against blacks in South Africa. He would do it, he said, but the problem would never come up. The general's transparent enthusiasm gradually disarmed his critics. One student asked, "You are obviously a patriotic man. What can you say to convince us that we should be as patriotic?" Chappie replied, "I can only tell you the way that I feel. Although I admit that there are many things wrong with America, there are less things wrong with her than in any other country. I still feel the question of racism is soluble here, and I think it can be solved without polarizing back into black and white." Although the president of the Afro-Union replied that most members of his organization did not share the general's views, he conceded that the membership, to their surprise, had come to recognize that General James was an "honorable man."[18]

As the episode at the Afro-Center at Wisconsin suggests, Chappie James became one of the government's most effective emissaries to black students. Young black school kids identified with him and his beribboned chest as "cool." They liked his quip, "Just because you are black, baby, don't mean they can't shoot your rear out of the sky." A friend who accompanied General James to a large black high school in Dallas marked by student unrest commented on his stunning effect on his audience:

While he spoke the auditorium was completely silent. He electrified these young people. When he finished they stood and cheered. An hour later, he was still standing on the stage, surrounded by young people who wanted to talk to him, or just to touch him. To them, he epitomized the fact that you can become anything you set out to be in this country. He was the most effective black spokesman for inspiring young people to constructive action that I have heard and I have heard them all.[19]

General James, listed in *Ebony* in the 1970s as one of its "100 Most Influential Black Americans," also appealed to a large number of educated, patriotic, and responsible blacks who proudly saw him as a symbol of opportunity and of the country's confidence in black leaders.[20] Mayor Johnny Ford of Tuskegee summarized this position when he remarked, "After Martin Luther King, Chappie was what was left of the dream. He was our symbol of hope because no other black leader was taking the position that we should all work for personal excellence and common humanity and America."[21] These blacks also admired James's service on behalf of Whitney Young, the Urban League leader who had died while attending a conference of black Americans and African leaders in Lagos, Nigeria. Chappie was assigned by President Nixon to return Young's body in Air Force Two. When the plane landed and the door came up, black civil rights leaders gathered with whites at the base of the ladder were said to be immensely comforted to see General James emerge from the cockpit as pilot.[22] Appreciation also was expressed by a black teacher who wished to give black students a better image of themselves. She placed all news of General James on her "Soul Corner" board and observed that students frequently stopped there and talked about him. She wrote, "Words are not adequate to express what we feel when we read of such wonderful accomplishments of one of our own."[23]

Another group that identified with General James was black servicemen who were increasingly numerous after the inception of the Volunteer Army in 1974. Not only did he exemplify opportunity for blacks in the military, but he also served their cause by refusing to encourage separatism despite racial unrest at military bases at that time. His speeches to blacks and whites in service expounded a philosophy of patriotism and professionalism before race. At Camp Pendleton in California he told 1,500 marines, several hundred of whom were black, "Racial problems are going to be solved by men and women who consider themselves Americans, not Africans." He instructed black cadets training in the F-4 similarly: "You are here to learn to fly this mother, and if you can't learn to fly it, out you go, and I don't care what color, creed, or what you are; your job is to fly the airplane."[24]

James often was repudiated by younger and more militant blacks, however, because he believed violent dissent by blacks was "sheer stupidity" and that militant leaders didn't know what suffering was because they were too busy making a career out of the movement.[25] To their complaints he would reply with a statement such as, "I know for my son and his young black contemporaries the way is much easier and the opportunity is there. If they are willing to work hard, they will make it."[26] The general's sleeplessness and upset stomach were often induced by clashes with the militants, yet he retained his outward calm and positive manner even at these difficult times. A favorite reply to the separatists or militants who accused him of being an "Uncle Tom" or at best a token was, "I came by these stars by working for them. . . . Nobody gave me anything, because I wouldn't accept it."[27] And when Tuskegee high schoolers greeted him at the airport on a visit to his alma mater with hand-raised, close-fisted salutes, he replied, "All right, now open your hands and tell me what you have got inside them."[28] Clearly, he was rejected by some black students on college campuses as well, yet he jocularly described their response: "I have had some [students] who say 'Oh Man' and get up and walk out. I can usually tell how many will walk out when I go in. Usually the one under that big hat trying to go to sleep. When I raise my voice, he opens one eye. When I say 'when that door of opportunity opens be ready,' he pulls that hat down. When I say 'black racism is as bad as white racism,' that's when he gets up and walks out . . . and one of those sisters chewing that gum then starts talking to a buddy and then all of a sudden is gone. She didn't want to listen in the first place."[29]

Curiously, the general experienced some of his worst criticism from blacks in his hometown, Pensacola, Florida, who apparently felt he was out of touch with them and with the problems of ordinary blacks outside the military. This attitude existed despite the fact that Chappie had demonstrated unusual powers to them in the area of military-civilian relations in 1970 when, much to his chagrin, after returning from Vietnam combat and tussles with Khadafy and after being designated by the Kiwanis Club of Pensacola as Man of the Year, he was denied entrance to what was then a celebrated "red-neck" bar in Pensacola. The incident was read into the *Congressional Record,* and the Torch Club was summarily declared, upon James's initiative and subsequent action by the Defense Department, off limits to military personnel, an action that deprived the club of a major source of its revenue. The incident also prompted local newspaper editor J. Earle Bowden to write an editorial deploring discrimination against James. The editor lauded James as a "big man" of whom all Americans may be proud and called for "those elements in our community still living in the past to take a new look at themselves" because the time had come "to end bigotry and racism."[30]

James's last major responsibility at the Defense Department was as liaison with the families of servicemen who were known prisoners of war or missing in action in Southeast Asia. The Johnson administration had not acknowledged the capture of those men, but Secretary Mel Laird insisted that the government go public in the interest of the men and the country, and the Nixon administration did so in 1969. (As of

September 1971, 465 Americans were listed as prisoners in Hanoi and 1,134 as missing.)[31] This policy incurred the risk of generating great sympathy for their distressed wives and families and possibly hastening America's withdrawal from Vietnam regardless of cost to national interest. But disclosure also presented the Nixon administration with opportunities. If world attention could be focused on the mistreatment of American prisoners, their plight might be improved and the resolve of the country strengthened to take all necessary action to achieve an honorable peace against an inhuman foe. These latter considerations prompted Secretary Laird to call attention to Hanoi's numerous violations of the Geneva Convention regarding the rights of American prisoners of war: parading them and forcing them to make propaganda statements, refusing to allow inspection of prison camps, and withholding a complete list of prisoners, especially those captured in South Vietnam and Laos.

The Defense Department's public affairs division took a leading role in organizing wives and families of POWs and MIAs. The National League of Families of American Prisoners and Missing in Southeast Asia, the principal organization for family members of POWs and MIAs, originated in a posh country club on the West Coast in the spring of 1970. No expenses were spared by the government to provide for the 100 or more guests, mostly wives, that day. Dan Henkin and General James were seated at the head table and both had expressed Secretary Laird's determination to bring pressure on Hanoi to fulfill the accords of the Geneva Convention. Suddenly one of the women ran tearfully out of the room. Others who were overwrought followed her and the mood became turbulent. General James got up and said, "Ok, that's enough. We can do two things—wrap ourselves in emotions and hysterics and attack the government or sit down and have a meeting of the minds." Referring to his son Danny, then flying in Vietnam, he said, "There isn't a night that goes by when the phone rings that my heart doesn't go thump, thump, too!" His presence of mind calmed the others and dialogue began.[32] Commitments were later made: families and wives would organize independently but would receive information and official help in drumming up public support, domestic and international, to improve the conditions of the POWs and secure their release. H. Ross Perot, a wealthy Texas oilman, supplied monies for the National League of Families, which also collected funds from its membership. That membership was restricted to family members (3,000 relatives)—that way, as one robust participant vouched, "we could best keep our virginity"—and a national headquarters was established in Washington.[33]

Although this unofficial linkage between the National League of Families and the Defense Department initially was welcomed by most POW-MIA relatives and wives, the alliance was often unsteady.[34] The Defense Department and the league both were interested in the release of the prisoners, but for the prisoners' wives and relatives that issue was preeminent, even exclusive, while the government sought other primary objectives as well: an independent South Vietnam, a program of effective Vietnamization in the South, and honorable withdrawal by American forces. The administration feared, of course, that league members out of frustration might contribute dramatically to the nation's antiwar stance.

General James's role as principal liaison between the Defense Department and the National League of Families was undoubtedly one of the most perplexing in his career. He was dealing with anxious women, and he was doing so as an official representative of the broader interests of the administration in the prisoner-of-war issue. His position that the women in the league were, after all, military wives and had to realize that their husbands ran risks of being captured and detained for long periods did not win him popularity.[35] Nor could the general respond affirmatively to their pressures to escalate the issue for immediate results (prisoners' release). Jerry Freidheim described James's dilemma: "Sometimes the government could respond. Sometimes it had to say no or ask for patience of folks out of patience. It fell to Chappie from time-to-time to say both yes and often no. Whenever any of us said no, some among the relatives felt us insensitive. We understood that. Part of Chappie's job was to help keep up relatives' morale; thus his times of having to 'let them down' a bit were harder for some relatives to take. He certainly was not insensitive. He held lots of hands and wiped lots of tears. He was compassionate; but he was not a psychologist or psychoanalyst by training. He was a warrior who on occasion must have thought that some of the prisoners would have wanted their relatives to press him less vigorously."[36]

James demonstrated both strengths and weaknesses of personality with the wives and relatives of the POWs as he kept them informed about policies in the White House and at the Defense Department affecting the POW-MIAs and gave numerous speeches throughout the country encouraging a letter-writing campaign to Hanoi to improve treatment of prisoners and to other foreign capitals to bring pressure on North Vietnam.[37] Comedian Bob Hope recalls General James's extraordinary public relations work on behalf of POWs one night in Houston in 1971: "There had been a lot of speakers that night and Chappie stood up in the middle of the room and said, 'a toast to our men in the Hanoi Hilton,' and a thousand people got up and toasted our prisoners."[38]

President Nixon, who came to know General James through his participation on a special White House committee, also retains very positive impressions of Chappie's overall service on POW-MIA matters "as the government's most effective spokesman in efforts to improve the conditions of captivity for our men held in North Vietnam. . . . He was articulate and forceful in stating their plight and concerns to the news media and to the Congress."[39]

One of General James's major accomplishments on behalf of the prisoners came in February 1972, when the prisoners finally returned to American soil. He had arranged for their transportation, new uniforms, medical assistance, and immediate hospitalization, and he safeguarded the rights of health and privacy of the returnees until they were able and ready to talk to reporters.[40]

James was not without his critics, however. Some women alluded to his partiality to air force prisoners and neglect of marine, navy, and army prisoners; one woman even went to the secretary of the army to have him reprimanded. Because this move represented a public repudiation, Chappie responded with an ugly temper. He told an assemblage of the women that no one worked harder for the POWs than he and he would appreciate disaffected persons coming to him first rather than going to superiors and hurting his career in the process. Career success was of course uppermost in the minds of many higher military officers, though it seems unlikely that it would preoccupy them to the point that they would declare their allegiance so bitterly over such a minor issue.

While at the Pentagon, James also gave a large number of speeches to citizen groups across the country. Because his audiences were generally conservative, they welcomed his patriotic speeches, which affirmed their beliefs in hard work, sacrifice, and excellence (James won the Horatio Alger national award in 1976) and encouraged them to keep faith in the future of the American system.[41] Although General James endorsed most features of the American way of life in these talks, he invariably drew attention to racial discrimination in the United States and denounced its practice.

When he spoke before the Daughters of the American Revolution convention in 1973, just thirty-four years after Marian Anderson had been denied an opportunity to sing in their sacred hall, he underscored that issue. In the words of Nick Thimmesch, a reporter covering the event, "Chappie looked like he could have been standing next to George Washington crossing the Delaware when he said, the military stood for peace, 'but if we must fight, we shall.'" The women "let out a roar" when James declared, "In the military our job is not to be popular, but to be strong." According to Thimmesch, "their eyes misted" when he remarked "This is my nation. I love her. If I see her ill, I will hold her hand." The women then became "ecstatic" as the general snapped to a salute when the organ struck up the Star Spangled Banner, just after his final remarks calling on the silent majority to speak up and be counted. But that was only part of the message. He complimented the women for "the progress that's very visible tonight as I stand here talking." But the general clearly also stated that everything was not right in the Republic and would not be until there was a cessation of hatred and intolerance and hence the coming of a united nation whose people would be so strong that they would be impervious to attack or subversion. It was not enough for those in the audience to say that they did not call others "niggers" or "honkies"; it was imperative that everyone became responsibly involved to see to it that equal opportunity became a fact of American life. According to Thimmesch, however, "The ladies still applauded with the zest of their forefathers."[42]

General James's contributions to the credibility of the Defense Department at a difficult time for the military were much appreciated by the civilian leaders in the Pentagon, especially Secretary of Defense Laird and two high officials in the public affairs division of the Defense Department, Dan Henkin and Jerry Freidheim. James's skills as communicator for the department primarily accounted for his rapid ascent from brigadier (one star) in 1970 to lieutenant general (three stars) in 1974. Besides, the strong impression he made on people would not allow him to be easily shelved. He also had the right friends, Melvin Laird and the assistant secretary of defense and later governor of Texas, William P. Clements. Laird was especially helpful because he held strong convictions about equal opportunity for deserving persons at the highest levels of the military, having recommended the first woman admiral as well as promotions for General James.[43]

General James's second star was contested by the air force. Dan Henkin requested that James be promoted because of his unusual skills at the Defense Department, but the initial response of the air force was that many other officers had precedence; in the early discussions, at least, it did not look like James would be promoted. Secretary Laird met with Air Force Secretary Robert C. Seamans, Jr., and Under Secretary John McLucas and insisted on the promotion, and the boards and review bodies concurred.[44] Chappie received his third star with slightly different players. Elliot Richardson was secretary of defense, Freidheim had replaced Henkin as assistant secretary for public affairs, and John McLucas was air force secretary. For the third and fourth stars, selection depended on specific assignments and was no longer the responsibility of the promotion boards. In other words, men holding the rank of lieutenant general or of general did so when there was a specific slot open for an officer to hold that rank. When Freidheim on Richardson's encouragement asked McLucas to promote Chappie to his third star because he was being nominated as principal deputy and number-two man at public affairs, the air force secretary responded that he would consider the possibility, but he noted that the air force did not pass out ranks to any but extraordinary airmen. Freidheim replied that Chappie was "extraordinary in every respect, in his service to the air force and also his service to the Department of Defense and the entire government," and the promotion came through. Freidheim recalls:

> When he was promoted to Lieutenant General, Chappie came into my office for a cup of congratulatory coffee and said, "I want to thank you for what you did about this." I told him he had done it not me, but that if either of us wanted to thank anybody we ought to thank his mother; he agreed and we toasted Mrs. James with Pentagon coffee.[45]

The fourth star would come only two years later, in 1975, when the command at the North American Air Defense came open. Secretary of Defense James Schlesinger and Air Force Secretary McLucas decided after lengthy deliberation that James was suited for the position.[46] The air force had some reservations because so many of Chappie's top promotions had been inspired by his successes in public relations rather than specific air force functions, but decided to go along. Chappie had received a strong recommendation from General P. K. Carlton for his work as Carlton's vice commander at the Military Air Lift Command after leaving the Pentagon in August 1974.[47] Besides, James had experience in the Air Defense Command after Korea and the air force felt he would be competent in that command, though strong support from Assistant Secretary Clements may have decided the issue at the last moment.[48] But for all that, it is unlikely Chappie James would have become a four-star general if it hadn't been for specific social problems in the early 1970s affecting the military for which his charisma and skills in mediation were peculiarly suited. His distinguished military record and ability to lead were responsible for his promotion to the rank of one-star general and helped justify later promotions, but it was his military-related rather than military skills that primarily accounted for his subsequent rise in rank. Just as Napoleon required the French Revolution to achieve prominence and glory, Chappie James's success rested on specific historical conditions. As a general capable of reconciling black and white, dissidents and majority, civilian and military, enlisted personnel and top brass during the troublesome late 1960s and early 1970s, Chappie was a consummate representative of the success formula of being the right person in the right place at the right time.

When James was about to get his fourth star, a colleague saw him in the Pentagon corridors one day and kidded him about who would pin on the fourth star. "Will it be President Ford? Or the chief of staff? Or someone else?"

General James lighted up, and he said, "No, listen, let me tell you about the ceremony. It will be on the steps of the Lincoln Memorial at high noon, starting with a flyover of fighter planes. Then I will step out, in chains, naked from the waist up. Then they'll break the chains, throw a blue cloak over my shoulders, and the D.A.R. chorus will sing the Battle Hymn of the Republic."

"You're sure that's not too low key?" the friend asked. "We're going to make a plus out of it," Chappie said, laughing to himself as he walked off down the hall.[49]

Dorothy James noted a special gleam in Chappie's eyes during the ceremony when the four stars were placed on each shoulder board. She felt he was saying to her with his eyes, "You see, I told you I could do it." He was probably also winking at Joe Morris, his boyhood friend whom he told he would be important some day, the high schoolers to whom he announced his intention to fly, the Tuskegee Airmen whom he promised he would make general, and the men in his squadron at Bentwaters who heard from him, "You can be as great and go as far as you want if you try hard enough."

Dorothy unquestionably was elated over her husband's success, but she well knew its cost to their family life. Chappie's demanding schedule—frequent twelve- to fifteen-hour days in the myriad activities and responsibilities he assumed while at the Pentagon—left him with very little time for his wife or family. Actually, that had been the case throughout his career. His needs for his family were subordinated to more insistent personal demands for performance and recognition in work and work-play, the latter involving keeping up the morale of his fellow air force officers, a task essential to his management successes. He often stated publicly his admiration for Dorothy's ladylike qualities, her taste in dress and decor, and her excellence as a mother. He also appreciated the fact that she was essentially unaffected. Unlike many generals' wives who manipulated others through such remarks as "my general wants" or "the general wants," she referred to Chappie publicly only as "my husband." He tried to protect her and her shyness as well when she experienced the sting of racist remarks from other officers' wives, at times unintended and at other times careless, though he ran out of patience when she was often late for social engagements or was indecisive about family plans. Chappie adhered to a sense of marriage as a polarized relationship, Dorothy responsible for home and family and he for their economic and social well-being. Separation stemming from perceptions of

The James family, 1975. Left to right: *Colonel Frank Berry, Danice James Berry, Claude James, General James, Dorothy James, Captain Daniel James III, and Berry grandchildren.*
(Courtesy of U.S. Air Force)

roles was reinforced by genuine differences in their personalities. At parties, they often were separated because he was as gregarious as she was reticent. Friends recall Dorothy at the officers' parties—quiet, dignified, reserved, usually with a small group of women—while Chappie was amid a large group of men and women, laughing, always laughing.

As Chappie advanced in rank and responsibility, his children, like his wife, were apt to see as much of him in public life as in their home, though one benefit of his incessant work ethic was that they met at home many of his air force friends, who became their friends as well. Chappie experienced conflict and guilt over raising the children, because he felt it imperative to transmit to them the same formula for achievement he had learned from his parents, but he was uneasy about taking time out from his career to spend the necessary time to do so. (Dorothy states that her chief task in marriage was to get her husband to slow down; she notes, "We had no time for family vacations.") James demanded much from his children, especially proficiency in school, and he suffered personally when his son Danny (Daniel James III) was forced to leave the Air Force Academy because of deficiencies in mathematics and when his younger son Claude dropped out of Florida State University with poor grades. But his affection for them was much stronger than his criticism, and he was proud of all three of his children: Danice, the only daughter, after graduation from Florida A & M University and a career as an airline stewardess, married air force physician Frank Berry. Danny became an air force captain and flew more than 300 combat missions in Vietnam and later became a pilot with Braniff and Continental airlines. Claude (or Spud), with whom Chappie conceded he had lost touch, was a member of the youth culture of the late 1960s and early 1970s but later became an army technician and a hospital technician after he was released from the service.[50]

10. The Last Command

Chappie James's last command at the North American Air Defense (NORAD) was located at Cheyenne Mountain in the Colorado Rockies. The command post itself, a vast electronic city, was hollowed from mountain rock and insulated against thermonuclear explosions by a futuristic apparatus of "blast doors," shock absorbers, and continuous, heavy, welded steel plates. As CINCNORAD (Commander in Chief NORAD), General James was responsible for the very issue of America's survival as a nation. He supplied information directly to the president of the United States on possible air or missile attacks on the country, and the gravity of that information was certain to affect the president's decision on appropriate reaction. His appointment as CINCNORAD, even more than his four-star rank, meant General James had attained a degree of public trust and confidence almost unique among blacks in the United States. As a consequence, he became in these last years of his life one of the country's most important spokesmen of biracial community. He dramatized for whites that blacks were deserving and for blacks that there was hope in the system. This role was not new, but at NORAD James conveyed that message from his most conspicuous and prestigious position of authority.[1]

The NORAD command operated one of the world's most comprehensive surveillance systems through an intricate web of early warning radar and sophisticated sensors. Its information gatherers identified aircraft, missiles, or space objects and tracked them with push-button speed on giant screens at its command post. Indeed, information from the Distant Early Warning Line, or the Greenland Ice Cap, or a ballistic missile early warning system in Alaska could be relayed on screens under Cheyenne Mountain entirely by computers without the need for any human contact in "real time," at only fractional differences from the time the object was first tracked by distant NORAD sensors. These findings then could be plugged into the nation's top defense circuits by instant hot-line communication to the Pentagon, the Strategic Air Command, Canadian Forces in Ottawa (NORAD was a joint American-Canadian defense operation), and the White House.[2]

The Cheyenne Mountain underground complex had become fully operational in 1966, in response to the extraordinary growth in nuclear ballistics capacity by the Soviet Union in the late 1950s and the 1960s. As a consequence the NORAD commander's major duties, at one time concerned exclusively with attack from Russian bombers, became surveillance for missiles and the interpretation of these threats for the national command in Washington and the president. As James described this responsibility, "Every time there is a cloud of dust in Russia we have to know what it is and where it is going."[3]

Chappie James brought special personal skills to the new assignment, especially in personnel management. He impressed those around him, once again, at all levels—the secretaries, aides, and higher officers—with his ability to personalize leadership. That style was evident after the change of command ceremony when he was formally installed as CINCNORAD by the air force chief of staff, General David C. Jones; the new four-star general walked out to the edge of the stage and gave a heartfelt smile and thumbs-up salute to a throng of friends and well-wishers.[4]

These same personal skills helped foster positive relations with Canadians who staffed and supported the NORAD command. NORAD, because of Canada's vulnerability to Soviet air and missile attack from the north, was Canada's

Official air force photograph of General James with four stars. James was presented his fourth star on 29 August 1975 from General David C. Jones.
(Courtesy of U.S. Air Force)

most important treaty; the NORAD commander required appointment by both the Canadian prime minister and the United States president. Lieutenant General William K. Carr, commander of the Canadian Forces Air Command during General James's tenure at NORAD, emphasized Chappie's "inspirational qualities" and at the same time "his deep sensitivity for all men," which "motivated the best in those he commanded."[5] General Carr underscored James's utility for the joint command by stressing his skills in communication with the Canadians.

> Chappie did much to cement even more firmly U.S.-Canadian relations, particularly in the field of military cooperation. His lucid and objective explanation of his job as he saw it was welcomed on more than one occasion on the Canadian TV networks. His explanation left little doubt about the value of mutual respect and its power as a cohesive force.[6]

General James's main "civilian activity" at NORAD was speech making. His reputation as a speaker together with the prestige of his command made him attractive to groups throughout the country. The topic, appropriately, of those speeches while James was CINCNORAD dealt almost exclusively with questions of national security, and their theme was that the United States must arrest the erosion of its military power brought on by disillusionment over Vietnam or confront a superior enemy that would exploit its weakness. During the summer of 1976 he was particularly critical of Democratic presidential candidate Jimmy Carter, who already had called for military cutbacks. Despite Carter's naval background, James insisted that "there were many things about defense he might not know about at this time." He then praised the incumbent: "My Commander in Chief is still Gerald R. Ford and he is not cutting the defense budget."[7] When cutbacks in defense spending came after Carter's election, General James continued to complain to friends, including former President Ford, about Carter's policies on defense, especially over the B-1, but he of course avoided ad hominem references in public about the new commander in chief and concentrated rather on winning friends for military preparedness.[8]

In his personal life James had emphasized strength and

determination to attain his objectives; as a general, speaking for the NORAD command, he was committed to the same values. Conversely, weakness and indecisiveness were deplorable to him, and this attitude too was objectified in his call for a stronger American defense. In speech after speech to civilians during the NORAD years (1975–1978) James was an unequivocal advocate of American power and national will to use that power when appropriate. He frequently cited the preponderant power of the United States at the time of the Cuban missile crisis to illustrate that peace depended on American power; President Kennedy was able to intimidate the Russians, who were forced to back down short of conflict.[9] He also disparaged the antimilitary, even pacifist spirit that had developed in the United States after the Vietnam War. He warned people who held such views that they might not appreciate the freedom that the United States provided until they lost it. He chastened them with indebtedness to John Stuart Mill: "War is an ugly thing, but not the ugliest thing, rather that decadent state of moral and patriotic feeling that nothing is worth fighting for." To which James added: "Those who subscribe to the pacifist view were only kept alive by persons much stronger and sacrificial than themselves."[10]

General James most clearly stated his thesis that American power was the guarantor of world peace and human freedom when he received the Man of the Year Award from the Doolittle Chapter of the Air Force Association in the spring of 1976. He declared:

> Power is an international language. Nobody needs a translator. Nobody wants to be a partner of a weakling. . . . We are not weak yet, but we have moved away from a position of strength. . . . We have gone closer to a state of parity which we think is acceptable to the people of the United States. But the danger here is that as you approach parity it is hard to stop the pendulum from swinging past center,

and then the balance of power shifts to those people who don't hear you at all. . . . Given the technology today if that pendulum swings too far there is no recovery. It makes the most deadly game we have ever engaged in. Too many people today take for granted our freedom, people of overstuffed abundance and people who say, "what is in it for me?" I would be less than candid if I said I was not alarmed by the number of people today who leap on the comparatively small number who speak of sacrifice to maintain our security forces so that they can fight to preserve our freedom.[11]

General James's responsibilities at NORAD with 20,000 American personnel under his charge, his visits to remote places in Greenland, Canada, and Alaska, the welcoming of visitors to Cheyenne Mountain, and his speech making, most of which was done after hours, on his own time, stretched his endurance to the breaking point. Dorothy James, herself not well at the time, conceded that she never could convince him to take a vacation, and aides repeatedly noted the general reading in the lighted back seat of his chauffered staff car on the way to NORAD headquarters at 6 o'clock in the morning and returning at 7:30 in the evening. One aide's wife complained bitterly when she had not seen her husband for forty-three days, time he spent on continuous trips with General James.[12] James also was affected by protracted controversy with the air force chief of staff, General David C. Jones, over the future of NORAD. Jones was intent upon restructuring and cutting back the NORAD command, parceling out more of its duties to the Tactical and Strategic Air Commands. An old fighter pilot, General James resented these decisions from the "bomber people" who had taken control with General Jones, and he called without success for an enlargement of the number of fighter planes operationally under his command. Despite General James's steadfast denials, syndicated columnists Robert Novak and Rowland Evans later would charge that he was forced to retire from the service prematurely on this account. The charge was irresponsible, but the two columnists did expose a heated dispute between the two generals.[13]

Such pressures and tensions easily could produce medical problems; Chappie James had been contesting a weight problem since his time at RAF Bentwaters, and he had a history of high blood pressure. Besides, the big general continued to live life to the fullest, enjoying parties, sporting events, singing at the officers' club, and relishing good food with an abundance of salt and especially his Tangueray. Aides were concerned about his drinking straight gin and sometimes would order scotch and water for him, but after one or two, he would turn and say, "OK, now where is the good news? Bring the Tangueray."[14]

In mid-September 1977, General James attended a Denver Broncos football game where he felt discomfort. He worked the following Monday but did not feel well. He was taken to the hospital at the Air Force Academy and was about to be discharged the following morning when a report on his enzyme level revealed he had experienced a "mild disabling coronary event."[15] The air force doctor asked him to remain in the hospital for observation and prescribed a liquid protein diet. James was hospitalized until November 3, losing twenty pounds over the six-week period. Despite the gravity of his health problems, he minimized them and remained something of a rogue. He tried to get some friends to smuggle some Tangueray into his hospital room and wrote a friend in the bakery business in Pensacola, promising a golf game and asking him "to send me some cakes and sweet rolls."[16] He was especially touched during his hospital stay by appreciative messages from the corps of cadets at the Air Force Academy.

Chappie never fully recovered from his heart attack. He pressed on thereafter to the limit of his abilities but he was often tired and groggy from medications. He managed to cohost a Sammy Davis, Jr., show on November 11 at the Air

Force Academy when Davis announced that he had come because of his long-lasting friendship with Chappie and dedicated a song to him "with all the love in [my] heart." Chappie joined Sammy on stage, despite his great fatigue, because he too believed that the show must go on. That morning an aide, noting that he looked very pale, had asked him if he should attempt the appearance on stage. Chappie looked in the mirror and commented, "You know that white boy sees things I don't see," the invariable humor surfacing even then.[17]

General James was scheduled to retire on May 1, 1978, but his heart condition prompted an earlier retirement on medical disability on February 2, 1978.[18] He proposed his own resignation to General Jones and accepted a limited duty assignment from December 7, when he stepped down from NORAD. He had no regrets over the thirty-five years of service to his country. As he later remarked, "If I could write the script for my life all over again, of how I wanted it to go, I don't know of anybody else who has, to a greater degree, been able to do precisely what he wanted to do and what he had the most fun doing and that he felt the most sense of accomplishment at having done than I have. The Air Force is the greatest place in the world for me, and if I had to do it all over again, I would do it exactly the same."[19] What he regretted most was stepping out of his uniform. Although he occasionally had been mistaken in a civilian airport for an airline baggage attendant by an unwitting traveler, it was "the uniform that assured him his best treatment" everywhere. After retirement, he might be exposed to occasional embarrassment, as on the day he was golfing with Jerry Pate and Coach Bear Bryant of Alabama and was mistaken in the clubhouse as a custodian.[20] And civilian dress meant driving his own car again and carrying his own bags and doing without all the perquisites of being a general.

Chappie was not a person who dwelt on the past, however. He was a long-distance runner who hardly could permit himself to fall out no matter how consuming the race. His conscious anticipation of civilian life was positive, and there seemed to be many good reasons for him to be optimistic. His retirement salary would be substantial. He was being courted by two gubernatorial candidates from Florida who wanted him to run as their lieutenant governor. At least two major corporations were negotiating with him to accept memberships on their boards of directors for handsome salaries. He also was considering purchasing a home on lovely Bayou Texar in Pensacola. It appealed to him for several reasons, one being that he wished to run his boat in an area where he would have been forbidden access as a boy. At least two prospective authors were discussing writing his biography and First Artists was negotiating for a film. Life would not be boring because he intended, he said, to campaign for outspoken advocates of American defense and for candidates, white and black, who would pledge to work to improve opportunities for poor people. And, of course, there would be more time for golf.[21]

On the morning of General James's retirement, he was invited by President Carter to the White House for a chat and picture taking. The two smiled broadly at one another and Carter reminded newsmen that the general had shared "an equal authority" with him while at NORAD, including responsibility for "initiating an atomic attack." He saluted James as a superb military officer in times of peace or war.[22] The retirement ceremony was held at Andrews Air Force Base, January 26, 1978. The spectacle was one that Chappie had witnessed many times for others, and few things appealed more to him than a good military show.[23] The Air Force Band was there and it primed the mood for the occasion with some stirring music. Guests rose during the band's presentation of "Ruffles and Flourishes" and the "General's March." An honor guard drill team stepped smartly to sharp commands, and officers then ceremoniously inspected the troops before General James, Secretary of Defense Harold Brown, and other dignitaries who watched from a flag-draped speaker's platform. Even these activities, which Chappie ordinarily relished, could not conceal the pain that stole across his face.[24] He was leaving his "beloved Air Force."[25] But ever since the days at Miz Lillie A. James's school, Chappie knew that he had to perform when the curtain went up for the annual play on graduation night, so he was ready, though highly charged emotionally, and when it came time for him to speak, he began in characteristic booming voice, "My mother told me, among many other bits of valuable philosophy, a very simple charge, as she pinned on my wings the day I earned them on a red clay hill in Tuskegee, Alabama, under tough conditions, and she said, simply, 'Do well, my son.'" At that point his voice cracked and became much more subdued. He continued, "The president of the United States, my commander in chief, said to me this morning, simply, 'Well done.' I think my mother heard him." Now his old exuberance and confidence were back. He concluded with a typical flourish to great applause, "Thank God for the United States of America. Thank God for the United States Air Force to keep her free. And thank you for giving me this honor. And God bless all of you."[26]

Defense Secretary Harold Brown in praising General James at his retirement ceremonies had good reason to observe that the four-star general would, as a civilian, merely be beginning a new phase of his traditional "active behavior."[27] Chappie scheduled several speeches and television talk shows on his favorite subjects, defense and equal opportunity, almost immediately after he became a civilian and awaited a call to serve on the board of directors for the Southern Railroad.[28] He admitted that he found civilian life "a little strange." While in Washington he called a close friend's wife and professed with chagrin that being a civilian was not easy. He was at the National Airport and had a flat tire. He also had left the lights on in the car and now it would not start. "Can you imagine," he remarked plaintively, "I have forgotten how to do these things."[29]

His speaking schedule led to visits to Milwaukee and Colorado Springs, where he was to speak to the American Trucking Association in late February. Before he departed, he visited Dottie, who was temporarily crippled with rheumatoid arthritis in a hospital at Andrews Air Force Base. He seemed to be anxious to get on with his new assignments, but he took time to be playful and embraced and kissed her and expressed hope that she would be feeling well by the time he returned.[30]

The "family" from NORAD was waiting at the Colorado Springs airport February 24, 1978, for the return of the "Chief"—David Swennes, Art Ragan, Cato Reeves, and Clark Price, all former aides except for Price, who was a fighter pilot and close to Chappie since their days at Bentwaters. They hid around the corner as General James descended. The "Chief" was wearing a three-piece blue suit with a pale yellow plaid vest. He grimaced when he found no one to meet him after deplanement. When the family appeared, he chided them, "Nobody can keep to a schedule anymore. Things have already gone downhill since I have left this place."[31] Despite the opening sally, however, he was not his usual self. He was tired and had left the pills for his heart ailment at home. He drove with Colonel Price to Peterson Air Force Base, obtained the prescribed pills, and then dined with a small company of friends. He complained of nausea and chest pain, so an ambulance was called from the Air Force Academy hospital. He was declared dead on arrival at the hospital at 2 A.M. February 25.[32]

The last wheels-up came the next morning when his body was flown from Colorado Springs to Andrews Air Force Base outside the national capital. Two generals, one, the black William Earl Brown, Jr., informed Dottie of the sad event; she responded instinctively, "Oh God, not my husband!"[33] General James's friends also reacted disbelievingly at first, as if it were inconceivable that such a vital man should die. Golfer Lee Elder asked Rose, his wife, who first told him the news, "Are you sure it's Chappie?"[34] Curt Smothers, the general's counselor who had been planning for Chappie's retirement with attractive business offers, broke down with grief. He knew it meant the end of his closest and dearest friendship and also the end of a great black hope in the American system. After their initial shock and sorrow, Chappie's friends responded in a manner that would have won approval from "the Chief." They provided a reception for the hundreds of persons who came to Washington for the funeral and lodgings and commiseration for the general's family from Florida. They also, of course, offered comfort to the bereaved immediate family, Dottie, still unwell, and the three James children.[35]

Preparations were made for a funeral mass at the Shrine of the Immaculate Conception and interment at Arlington National Cemetery. The former was a stately high mass attended by 1,500 persons, not the typical religious service for a deceased general, rather more akin in ceremony and trappings to those for presidents or cabinet members.[36]

The diverse group of people attending the requiem mass were united by their respect for the man they all called "Chappie." Congressional figures, cabinet and former cabinet members, and high-ranking military officers occupied the front pews. The rest of the congregation was made up of middle-grade officers and civil servants, large numbers of enlisted personnel, secretaries, and persons from all strata of society, many coming from such distant states as Texas and California as well as from Washington, D.C. At communion during the service, a two-star general was observed kneeling beside an enlisted man, a woman in a full-length silver-fox coat beside a man in a threadbare sweater. The great number of commoners present illustrated feelings of kinship with Chappie, whom they knew also had come from out of the ranks. Others remembered him who could not attend. All state office buildings in Florida flew their flags at half-mast on Wednesday, March 2, and the flag at Pensacola City Hall similarly was lowered by order of Mayor Warren Briggs.[37]

Chief of Air Force Chaplains Major General Henry J. Meade captured the mood of the congregation in his eulogy. Meade referred to Chappie's "infectious spirit," his service to the nation in helping to overcome "the agonies of mistrust, separation and division," and "his life story as a thrilling account of one person's ability to rise above all adversity and become an example of excellence."[38]

The general's body lay in state after the service in the shrine that night, attended by a color guard. Hundreds of persons filed by. Dottie herself noted with relief amid overwhelming sorrow that "he looked like he was at least getting some of the rest he so badly needed."

The following morning was sunlit and crisp. Spectators stood ten deep around the artillery caisson with its six magnificent, matched black horses before it set out for the gravesite. Approximately five thousand persons then watched the most ceremonious of American funerals—interment with military honors—the steady, solemn, sepulchral cadence of horses and riders moving to an appointed destination, the "riderless horse," the three rifle volleys, the folding of the flag over the casket and its presentation to the widow, the folding of the general's personal four-star flag, taps, and then that final moment of the ceremony—the awesome quiet. The dignitaries were there again, including Vice President Walter Mondale, Defense Secretary Harold Brown, Melvin Laird, Donald Rumsfeld, and Senators Barry Goldwater and John Tower, and so were the interesting assortment of people whom Chappie had touched—the well-dressed and fashionable men and women, black and white, and the large numbers who felt a trifle cold.

Chappie James would have approved of an editorial in the *Washington Post* dedicated to his memory the following morning. It stated:

> There was a kind of rock-ribbed Americanism about General James—a patriotism and a sense of gratitude that some found incongruous in a man who in childhood had known poverty and segregation first-hand. But there was really nothing incongruous about it. Chappie James simply possessed two

Grave site of General James in Arlington National Cemetery on day of his burial, March 2, 1978. (Courtesy of U.S. Air Force)

qualities that nurtured his patriotism and powered his truly remarkable advancement to the top of the nation's military structure: An indomitable will to succeed and, with it, a profound sense of appreciation of the special opportunity his country offered him—whatever its flaws. There will be many tributes to General James, but we think none will more eloquently characterize him than the words he once used to describe himself. "I am," he said, "above everything else . . . an American."[39]

He would have enjoyed other tributes as well. Roy Wilkins, leader of the NAACP, declared:

Daniel James—patriot, soldier, general, the black youth who dreamed of the seemingly impossible— has left an example of achievement for all youth, black and white. For his country he has left a record of patriotism and service of which all Americans can be proud.

Who would have thought it possible that Daniel James, a black youth who entered a segregated pilot training program unit at a time when the Army brass felt that blacks could not learn to fly, would be retired as a four-star general in the Air Force?[40]

A black airman who had never met General James summed it up only slightly differently in a letter to the *Air Force Times:*

General James may be remembered as the first black four-star officer, but I shall remember him as someone who inspired me to be proud I am an American and that although my roots may be elsewhere, there is no reason why I should not love America as he did.[41]

And from Melvin Laird, his leader and friend: "Chappie James was a man who gave his all for his country. He fought a tireless battle for the nation's strength and for equal opportunity for all."[42]

11. Conclusion

Daniel "Chappie" James, Jr. (1920–1978), the seventeenth
child in a black laborer's family in Pensacola, Florida,
achieved unprecedented distinction as the first of his race to
hold four-star rank as a general officer in the American military. He also had enjoyed public trust and confidence in a
broad spectrum of the population as had only few blacks in
American history. While his life was another Horatio Alger–type narrative, it was seemingly more true to that genre
and hence more poignant than many success stories because
of the formidable handicaps that region, social prejudice,
and tradition imposed. On the surface, at least, these obstacles would appear overwhelming, prohibitive to all claims
that he might become one of the eminent black Americans of
his time. He was raised in a black neighborhood in a small
southern city, with limited opportunities for socialization
and sophistication. His large family and his father's impe-
cunious occupation also suggested restricted opportunities.
Later, Chappie attended though did not graduate (until 1969)
from Tuskegee Institute, a college with a good reputation but
one that hardly assured personal success.

James's character, which accounted for his accomplishments, was profoundly influenced by his parents, especially
his mother. Lillie A. James was a forceful, demanding parent
who came from a black social class that had become highly
acculturated in the work ethic and other values of leading
white families in Pensacola. This group also recognized its
advantages over ignorant black migrants moving to the Gulf

Coast from farming areas in Alabama and was determined to maintain those advantages. Mrs. James established a private school with exacting standards of performance for her own children and others whose parents believed that a superior education for blacks would compensate for their disadvantages of race and color. She insisted that her students and especially her children could indeed realize their dreams in the United States if they had skills and if they developed attitudes and social conduct that would win the respect of whites. As a youth Chappie James was told repeatedly, at home and in school, that he would succeed if he were able to deprive whites of their negative stereotypes of blacks. He also learned that it was important that he demonstrate personal reliability in supporting the society's paramount values, such as patriotism. Young James also was taught to have confidence in authority and to believe that if he passed society's tests by developing personal qualifications he would be generously rewarded. Unquestionably, James's father, Daniel Sr., also served as an important model of hard work and discipline. Chappie had been schooled to work hard and to work within the social system.

While the logic of Chappie James's education at home was certain to win favor for him once he embarked on a career in the military, its emotional consequences would heighten that effect dramatically. His mother's insistence on rigorous and perfectionistic standards in education and morals for her students and especially her own children, whom she instructed at home as well as at school, powerfully affected Chappie's personal development. Although he would rebel in adolescence against her regimen that emphasized bookish achievements, preferring instead a heroic ideal and activities that required great strength and daring, he did not depart from her basic message: survival and success in a world dominated by whites required extraordinary achievements by blacks. Because Mrs. James reinforced that message by bestowing rewards conditional upon the youngster's willingness to internalize her prescriptions, he felt a special urgency to oblige her. He probably perceived that his mother's affection toward him was dependent upon his striving, indeed upon his achieving. The combined effect of her rhetoric demanding exceptional performance in her children and her manipulative child raising would unleash incredible energies in her son. As an adult Chappie James often was described by persons who knew him well as a "bigger than life character" or as a "black John Wayne" not because of his size, which was large, to be sure, but rather because of his extraordinary desire to demonstrate mastery or potential for mastery over life. In his adult years this compulsion led to hypertension, sleeplessness, and perhaps premature death. The fact that he was uncertain whether he was doing enough, as defined by the exorbitant expectations of his mother when he was a child, was a major source of the drive that would impress many contemporaries. Chappie's need for distinction was accompanied, after he became successful, by expectations for recognition and appreciation by others—the rewards he originally sought from his mother when a youngster. Gratification also required, of course, sensitivity on his part to the needs of his mother and to others from whom he sought approval, and he developed that quality to an unusual degree. His mother's role in responding to the social and educational needs of the black community in Pensacola may have served as an exemplary model in deepening his awareness of the needs of others.

Given Chappie James's determination to lead and excel in manly pursuits and his skills in interpersonal relations, the United States Air Force provided James with a highly desirable career outlet, though he first had to surmount the obstacles posed by racial bigotry in the military service. He was forced to serve in segregated units at a time when there was general suspicion among higher officers in the air force as to the quality of black aviators and when promotions of black fliers were irregular and much below standard for time in service when compared with whites. As one of a small number of blacks retained as fighter pilots in integrated squadrons, Chappie was forced to confront in the 1940s and 1950s—official policies calling for integration of the services notwithstanding—prejudicial commanding officers, the indignities of traveling in the South, denial of housing and golfing privileges in the North, and snide looks and condescending gestures behind his back, especially from persons off base with whom he had to deal.

Chappie James fended these problems in a variety of ways. In Korea he established his qualifications as a fighter pilot, and with promotions he was given opportunity to demonstrate his remarkable leadership ability. James's style as a leader was marked by flair and bravado, patriotism, ability to inspire and convince others, an understanding of the feelings and motives of those who worked with and for him, and general willingness to administer loyally to their needs with personal warmth and an unfailing sense of humor.

James's rapid rise in ranks (lieutenant colonel in 1956, colonel in 1964), which distinguished him from other fighter pilots from Tuskegee with the exception of Benjamin O. Davis, Jr., was positively affected, of course, by increasing racial tolerance in the air force, but it came primarily from Chappie's abilities, especially his leadership and his determination to establish that a qualified black could force the system to be fair. While the major student of integration in the air force describes that process as "one of the great success stories of the civil rights movement," statistical data suggest that black officer contemporaries of James still were suffering some discrimination even in the 1960s. A report of the Air Force Equal Opportunity Conference as late as 1971 revealed that blacks constituted only .77 percent of the total officer strength in the air force above the rank of major. There was only 1 black general, General James, compared with 425 white generals and only 30 black colonels (up from 7 in 1967) while there were 6,310 white colonels.[1] Furthermore, only 1.7 percent of officers attending air force staff and leadership schools were black, and in 1972 at the Air War College, the premiere school for future higher officers, only 1 in 230 officers was black while the Air Command and Staff College was without a single black officer in 1970–1971.[2]

Chappie James simply had refused to allow race to interfere with his sense of eligibility as "the best" or "one of the best." Indeed, his race may have inspired him to greater success. A close friend during James's years in the Pentagon and at NORAD speculates that James's blackness may have inspired in him even greater drive "like a one-legged man gets satisfaction from trying to beat two-legged men in a race. It was one more challenge that showed how good he was."[3] The young black closest to General James in the 1970s, his lawyer Curt Smothers, concurs that his drive to excel was dictated partly by a conscious responsibility to blacks everywhere. "That mission to be equal in dignity and capacity with the very best whites made him bigger than life," Smothers says. "I don't know where he got that confidence, but he was determined never to let the race number get on top of him."[4]

While the air force obviously provided James with an opportunity to serve as a warrior and as a leader of warriors, it provided for other tangible needs in his character. Chappie sought to be rewarded by the recognition and praise that attended distinction and power, needs he felt ever since the days he first attempted to satisfy his mother's extraordinary early expectations of him. While he strove mightily to succeed and coveted his stars, it is doubtful that he sought promotions primarily for reasons of power or money. If money were his goal, he could have retired after his first star and been handsomely rewarded as a consultant for defense-related industries or even as a member of business directorates. If power were the dominant drive, there is little evidence that he inspired fear in others. On the other hand, he greatly enjoyed presiding at ceremonies, speaking in uniform with the spangled, multitiered rows of ribbons, and the "perqs" that accompanied his rank at the offical greetings and farewells at military bases as he came and departed with his staff car bedecked with blue flag and white stars. He also demanded much attention socially. His speaking and singing skills provided abundant attention and enthusiastic responses, and both were like sustenance to him. While at NORAD he had his own band and was, in the words of one aide, "in hog's heaven" despite veiled criticism that it was unbecoming to hear a four-star general singing songs like "Mack the Knife," "Feelings," and "After the Lovin'."[5] Sammy Davis, Jr., speculated that James would rather have been a singer—an exaggeration, but an insightful observation.[6] Few general officers paraded such arrays of plaques and trophies in their offices as did Chappie. These ranged in importance from framed letters from local chambers of commerce to awards from governors and commendations from national civic and philanthropic organizations. He was sensitive to slights or improper recognition when, for example, the crowds were too small or the introductions were unsatisfactory, and he became very displeased if an aide talked back while being dressed down.[7]

Despite his remarkable service record, his high visibility as a fighter pilot who had flown in Vietnam, his extensive public speaking and reception by President Johnson in the White House, and creditable performance in closing down Wheelus AFB in Libya without succumbing to pressures from Khadafy, James well might have retired from the military as just one more black colonel. His promotion to brigadier general (1970) and then extraordinary progress to four-star general (1975) reflected James's importance to his civilian superiors in the Pentagon; they recognized the special value of his service to the nation during the tumultuous period of the late 1960s and early 1970s. Thus, Chappie James's personal gifts as a reconciler of persons, black and white, civilian and military, became especially important when history made them useful. Although those superficially familiar with his career would emphasize merely his role as warrior, ultimately he was even more important as a unifier and as bearer and spokesman for the dream of the United States as a land of equal social opportunity.

For many blacks James's career, including the great command at NORAD, symbolized opportunity and trust on the part of whites. For whites General James's record and speeches also afforded confidence in a workable democratic biracial community at a time when there were troublesome signs that the United States might be coming apart racially. From James they learned that responsible blacks embraced patriotism and wished to work constructively toward a solution of the nation's social problems. Most of his presentations stressed that the United States was the greatest country in the world and "that it had worked hard to put right the inequities that existed before," but "there was still work to be done" and "everyone should become responsibly involved" to see to it that complete equality of opportunity would soon become a fact of American life.[8]

Because "unity in the principles of democracy and respect for one another's human dignity is our greatest weapon in America," James admonished blacks as well as whites when he believed that they interfered with the realization of those goals.[9] He counseled black militants "not to go back under that separate but equal blanket by asking for a separate this and separate that . . ." but rather to "reach out to those who are reaching out their hands to you . . . and a lot of those hands are white . . . they find it pretty hard to grasp hold if your hand is drawn tightly into a fist of hate. Togetherness, yes. Pride, yes. Hate, separatism, polarization, never."[10]

The general held out as the alternative to separatism "the power to excellence" and "the will to achieve in an integrated country." He declared, years before the Reverend Jesse Jackson developed similar themes in PUSH (People United to Save Humanity), that hard work and the cultivation of excellence were keys to the betterment of blacks because whites eventually would acknowledge those abilities and support, as a result, fair laws that would assure just treatment for all.[11] To the separatists who focused on past ills, Chappie juxtaposed "the bright promise of the present and the future." The past for him served merely as a reminder of how far blacks had come. He told blacks he was not so much impressed with the fact that "once there were none" as "now there are some."[12] He loved to direct his audience's attention to the Pensacola of his youth, with its segregated benches in parks and schools and public rest rooms ("Everywhere I looked this built-in inferiority complex for a young black lad growing up was evident"),[13] but all those signs of discrimination had passed and he himself had been honored by his hometown with a Chappie James Day and parade as well as the friendship of many of its prominent citizens.[14]

James's self-help philosophy for blacks also was aimed at teaching social unity. For the government to accord blacks special treatment was to deny them the equality they could earn in fair competition with whites. The government's role in a just society was merely to assure that relatively equal conditions existed for the contest, hence the need for integrated schools, full and equitable civil rights for all, and opportunities for all through such vehicles as job training programs.

General James believed that whites hostile or intolerant toward blacks were also destructive of social unity as were those who were sympathetic to fairer treatment of minorities but who refused to participate in political or social action that would afford blacks chances for self-fulfillment. He felt whites should not only open the door for qualified blacks but also help them as well as indigent whites to qualify, and that whites should search their hearts and then elect representatives "who would legislate equal opportunity and provide programs to give people a little head start when they were coming up in their formative years."[15] The general despised, however, quota systems for blacks to assure their success because these violated his commitment to individualistic excellence and the heroic style. He reminded his white audiences, "I don't want any percentages but I want you to make damned sure that opportunity is there. . . . I want blacks to be able to take part in that system of free enterprise. We still don't have enough black doctors, lawyers, managers, enough black laborers whose human dignity is protected by an honest paycheck because there is no opportunity." Poor blacks and poor whites who wanted to work also deserved programs that would help them to become employable. While the general did not expect injustices over race to disappear quickly, he was confident that greater improvements were in store: "It's going to take a little more time to get it together." The rewards for American society, he asserted, would be worth the required sacrifices.[16]

General James also attempted to effect consensus among divisive social groups on the issue of the role of the United States in Vietnam. In thousands of speeches between 1967 and 1968 and from 1970 to 1975, delivered with great effectiveness to hundreds of thousands of persons, he espoused the administration's position that U.S. military presence in Vietnam was justified and, later, that the United States should not withdraw until South Vietnam's independence was assured. Although he may have been the most convincing military leader espousing this view and hence one of the few effective persons to bridge the mutual mistrust between military (conservative) and civilian (liberal) societies in that period, the pendulum had already swung on that issue to the side of war weariness and rapid withdrawal of American forces from Vietnam.

Chappie James was offended by those who regarded him to be an "Uncle Tom" because he was an advocate of racial reconciliation and the promise of "the good life" for all Americans or because he supported the conservative and promilitary side of the debate on Vietnam.[17] He surely would have taken issue as well with those who would see his achievements in the military as a mere token offered to a black in a dangerous profession while blacks were denied similar opportunities in more socially desirable areas of management. Such inferences miss the mark in an assessment of James's career and accomplishments. He became a great man in the military because he was schooled to do so and had the right personal qualities to succeed. And the military, in an expression of a changing and more unified nation, saw fit to acknowledge his contributions.

General James was buried in Arlington National Cemetery on a prominent knoll shaded by maples, beeches, and oaks. The headstones for his new battalion were in long and straight rows. Less than a mile away within easy view lay the Pentagon, the scene of his most productive and successful years. Overhead could be heard the familiar, continuous sound of jet aircraft on their way to National Airport. The Black Eagle was at rest, but before he landed he had demonstrated remarkable things about the potential of the human spirit and about the evolution of a nation that had nurtured that spirit.

Notes

Introduction

1. Charles S. Johnson, *Growing Up in the Black Belt: Negro Youth in The Rural South* (Washington, 1941), pp. 316–17; Richard Wright, *Black Boy: A Record of Childhood and Youth* (1945; reprint ed., New York, 1966), p. 65.

2. Theodore Rosengarten, *All God's Dangers: The Life of Nate Shaw* (New York, 1975), pp. 97–343.

3. An Act to Authorize the President to Appoint General Omar N. Bradley to the Permanent Rank of General, *Statutes at Large* 64, A 224 (1950–1951). General Omar N. Bradley held five-star rank in peacetime but only as a result of a special act of Congress.

Chapter 1

1. Booker T. Washington, *The Negro in Business* (Boston, 1907) p. 230.

2. *Pensacola Daily News,* Apr. 17, 1900, p. 4.

3. Donald M. Bragaw, "Status of Negroes in a Southern Port City in the Progressive Era: Pensacola, 1896–1920," *Florida Historical Quarterly* 51 (January 1973): 287.

4. *Pensacola Florida Sentinel* (annual trade edition), May 26, 1906. Booker T. Washington declared that blacks in Pensacola paid taxes on property valued at $450,000. He described their homes as attractive and modern. See Washington, *Negro in Business,* p. 231. See also Charlene H. Hunter, *A History of Pensacola's Black Community* (Pensacola, 1971).

5. Wiggins's *Pensacola City Directory* (Columbus, Ohio, 1903), pp. 353–71.

6. Robert Bradley, "White-Black Residential Maps of Pensacola, 1905–1940" (History Department research paper, May 15, 1973, University of West Florida, in author's possession).

7. Author's interview with Napoleon Rancifer, Apr. 13, 1973. Rancifer, a waiter at the Pensacola Country Club and a lifelong resident of Pensacola,

was one of the social leaders in Pensacola's black community in the 1970s.

8. One older black resident recalls that a white man gave up his seat on a trolley car for his mother at this time. Author's interview with Rex Harvey, Apr. 17, 1973. "Colored patrons" of the Opera House were moved upstairs in 1901. See *Pensacola Daily News,* Aug. 29, 1901, p. 5.

9. *Twelfth Census of the United States, 1900, Population, I* (Washington, D.C., 1901), pp. 441, 612. There were 9,182 blacks in Pensacola in 1900 and 8,561 white citizens.

10. Author's interviews with Corrine Jones, Rosebud Robinson, Rex Harvey, and T. H. McVoy (older social leaders in Pensacola's black community in the 1970s), Apr. 17, 1973.

11. Ibid. The boll weevil disease affecting Alabama seriously in 1908, plus the pull of Pensacola's expanding economy, may have pushed whites and blacks into Pensacola.

12. *Fourteenth Census of the United States, 1920, Population, II* (Washington, D.C., 1921), p. 77. The census shows 20,631 whites and 10,404 blacks.

13. Pensacola's ordinance on racial separation on trolleys (whites riding in the front and blacks in the rear of the cars) apparently predated a similar state law. See Pauli Murray, *States' Law on Race and Color* (Cincinnati, 1951), p. 77. See *Pensacola Journal,* Oct. 14, 1905, p. 1. See "Conductor's Rules" to operate trolleys and insure segregation in *Pensacola Journal,* July 1, 1905, p. 5.

14. Jones, Robinson, Harvey, and McVoy, Apr. 17, 1973.

15. Bradley, "White-Black Residential maps."

16. *Pensacola Journal,* Feb. 24, 1911, p. 4.

17. Ibid., Jan. 4, 1911, p. 6.

18. Ibid., Oct. 10, 1909, p. 5.

19. Donald M. Bragaw, "Loss of Identity in Pensacola's Past: A Creole Footnote," *Florida Historical Quarterly* 50 (April 1972): 414–18. The year 1910 was "the cut-off date" for Creole listings in the city directory.

20. *Pensacola Journal,* July 30, 1908, pp. 1, 2, 3; Aug. 1, 1908, pp. 3, 5, 8; Aug. 2, 1908, p. 1; Aug. 4, 1908, p. 2. Pensacolians also mailed cards depicting Nate Shaw's riddled body. Ibid., Aug. 5, 1908, p. 5.

21. Jones, Robinson, Harvey, McVoy, and Muriel Brown (a teacher and elder citizen in Pensacola's black community), Apr. 17, 1973.

22. Author's interviews with Dr. Thomas James, Dec. 15, 1980, and July 18, 1983. Dr. James is a nephew of Chappie James, seven years his junior, and was raised in the same household.

23. Author's interview with Lillie James Frazier, Feb. 12, 1981. Mrs. Frazier is Chappie James's sister.

24. Author's interview with Gloria Hunter (niece of Chappie

James), June 10, 1980; Mabel W. Bates (niece of Mrs. Lillie James and student at her school) to author, July 14, 1980; Dr. S. W. Boyd (James family physician) telephone interview with author, Nov. 10, 1980; Frazier, Feb. 12, 1981.
25. T. James, July 18, 1983.
26. Frazier, Jan. 20, 1981.
27. Bates to author, July 14, 1980.
28. Frazier, Jan. 20, 1981.
29. Author's interview with Walter Richardson, Mar. 16, 1981. Richardson was also a student at Mrs. James's school. Note General James's remarks about his mother in *Kansas City Star,* Nov. 20, 1975 (copy in General James Scrapbooks, Tuskegee Institute Archives, vol. 16).
30. Frazier, Feb. 20, 1981.
31. Hunter, June 10, 1980; Bates to author, July 14, 1980; Boyd, Nov. 10, 1980; Frazier, Feb. 12, 1981.
32. Frazier, Jan. 12, 1981; author's interview with Maudeste James, Jan. 10, 1981. Maudeste James is an aunt of General James.
33. See speech of General James, San Diego, California, Mar. 18, 1972, in James Scrapbooks, vol. 11.
34. Frazier, Jan. 12, 1981. Estimates vary on the number of children in the James family. Vital statistics in Escambia County, Florida, Health Center, Pensacola, record twenty children born to Mrs. James by the time Dan. Jr. was born in 1920. At that

time, Dr. Herbert L. Bryan, the attending physician, reported that only seven of the James children were still alive.
35. T. James, Mar. 20, 1981. Dr. James is the son of Tony and Maudeste James. A former naval officer, he is a dentist who resides in Miami, Florida. M. James, Jan. 10, 1981; Frazier, Jan. 10, 1981; Hunter, June 10, 1980; records of vital statistics, Escambia County, Florida, Health Center.
36. Bates to author, July 14, 1980.
37. These observations about Chappie James were made to author by his sister, Lillie James Frazier, Jan. 10, 1981; his wife, Dorothy Watkins James, Sept. 3, 1980; Assistant Defense Secretary Dan Henkin, Dec. 28, 1981; and General James's fellow officer, Brigadier General James T. Boddie, Jr., Feb. 18, 1983.
38. Bates to author, July 14, 1980.
39. Author's interview with Joe Morris, Mar. 10, 1981.
40. T. James, July 18, 1983.
41. Material on Daniel James's high school years was supplied by interviews with his classmates Gloria McMillan, Dec. 15, 1980; Richard Crenshaw, Dec. 27, 1980; Lucille Galry, Jan. 5, 1981; Marie Davis, Jan. 5, 1981; Joe Morris, Mar. 10, 1981; and his principal, Vernon McDaniel, Jan. 18, 1981.
42. T. James, Mar. 20, 1981, and July 18, 1983.
43. Frazier, Feb. 20, 1981. On Chappie's fears that he might be forced to forgo college, see *St.*

Louis Globe Democrat, May 1–2, 1971, in James Scrapbooks, vol. 20.

Chapter 2

1. Good biographies of Booker T. Washington are Louis R. Harlan, *Booker T. Washington: The Making of a Black Leader, 1856–1901* (New York, 1972), and idem, *Booker T. Washington, Wizard of Tuskegee, 1901–1915* (New York, 1983). See also Robert L. Factor, *The Black Response to America* (Reading, Mass., 1970).
2. Author's interview with James Woodson, July 1, 1980. Woodson is a professor of history at Tuskegee and was a fellow student of James there.
3. *Tuskegana Year Book,* 1942, p. 34; author's interviews with James's Tuskegee classmates Claude George, Jan. 18, 1981; Wilbur George, Jan. 18, 1981; and T. C. Cotrell, June 30, 1980.
4. Author's interview with Robert Moore, June 30, 1980.
5. *Tuskegee Campus Digest,* Nov. 10, 1978, p. 2.
6. C. George and W. George, Jan. 18, 1981.
7. Author's interview with James's Tuskegee classmates Oscar "Tobey" Downs, Oct. 19, 1980, and C. George, Jan. 18, 1981.
8. D. W. James, Sept. 9, 1980.
9. Ibid.; USAF Biography, General Daniel James, Jr., Personal Fact Sheet, Albert F.

Simpson Historical Research Center, Maxwell Air Force Base, Montgomery, Alabama.
10. Moore, June 30, 1980.
11. Author's interview with "Chief" Charles A. Anderson, June 30, 1980. Chief Anderson directed CPT at Tuskegee. Lawrence J. Paszek, "Separate But Equal," *Aerospace Historian* 24 (September 1977): 136. See also Major Alan Gropman's interview with Brigadier General Noel F. Parrish, Mar. 30, 1973, Air Force Oral History Program, Simpson Research Center. See also Richard M. Dalfiume, *Desegregation of the U.S. Armed Forces: Fighting on Two Fronts, 1939–1953* (Columbia, Mo., 1969); William H. Hastie, *On Clipped Wings: The Story of Jim Crow in the Army Air Corps* (Washington, D.C., 1943); and Charles E. Francis, *The Tuskegee Airmen: The Story of the Negro in the U.S. Air Force* (Boston, 1955), pp. 12–15.
12. Anderson, June 30, 1980.
13. Ibid.; James Biography; author's interview with Colonel William Campbell (ret.), Apr. 10, 1983.
14. Author's interview with Colonel Hannibal Cox (ret.), Mar. 8, 1981. Colonel Cox is a former president of the Tuskegee Airmen, an association principally of fliers trained at Tuskegee. Noel F. Parrish to author, Jan. 19, 1981.
15. Alan M. Osur, *Blacks in the Army Air Forces During World War II* (Washington, D.C., 1977), p. 46.

16. Author's interviews with Tuskegee Airmen Charles E. Walker, Mar. 7, 1981; Hannibal Cox, Mar. 8, 1981; and Spann Watson, Mar. 15, 1981. Note also the remark by Lieutenant General Benjamin O. Davis, Jr., about the days of the segregated air force: "all the blacks in the segregated forces operated like they had to prove they could fly an airplane when everybody believed they were too stupid" (*New York Times*, Sept. 26, 1982, p. 33). William Campbell, another Tuskegee Airman, believes no one washed out of the flight program because he was black (Campbell, Apr. 10, 1983).

17. Gropman-Parrish interview; Parrish to author, Jan. 19, 1981.

18. For alleged racist remarks by a white flight instructor at Tuskegee, see *Dothan Eagle*, Mar. 12, 1978 (copy in James Scrapbooks, vol. 37).

19. Watson, Mar. 15, 1981; Walker, Mar. 7, 1981; and Cox, Mar. 15, 1981.

20. Cox, Mar. 22, 1981.

21. Francis, *Tuskegee Airmen*, p. 24.

22. Cox, Mar. 15, 1981; Watson, Mar. 15, 1981.

23. *Atlanta Journal*, Aug. 18, 1970; Cox, Mar. 15, 1981; Watson, Mar. 15, 1981; Walker, Mar. 7, 1981.

24. Osur, *Blacks in the Air Forces*, p. 45.

25. Ibid., pp. 48–51.

26. Alan L. Gropman, *The Air Force Integrates 1945–1964* (Washington, D.C., 1978), p. 14.

27. Osur, *Blacks in the Air Forces*, p. 130.

Chapter 3

1. Osur, *Blacks in the Army Air Forces*, p. 108. For the 477th Composite Group as a combined fighter and bomber unit (one fighter and two bomber squadrons), see "History of the 477th Composite Group," Sept. 15, 1945 to June 30, 1947, and "History of the 477th Bombardment Group (Medium)," Jan. 15, 1944 to July 15, 1945, Group Records, Simpson Research Center. The 477th Bombardment Group became the 477th Composite Group in September 1945. An excellent discussion of race relations in the air force during this period is Gropman, *Air Force Integrates*, pp. 86–142.

2. This is Osur's position in *Blacks in the Air Forces*, pp. 1–62 passim.

3. Ibid., p. 112.

4. Ibid., pp. 56, 112. Watson, Mar. 15, 1981.

5. Osur, *Blacks in the Air Forces*, pp. 52–53.

6. "History of the 477th Bombardment Group," Jan. 15 to July 15, 1949, p. 10.

7. Osur, *Blacks in the Air Forces*, pp. 54–57.

8. Major Alan Gropman's interview with Major General Daniel James, Jr., Oct. 2, 1973, Air Force Oral History Program, Simpson Research Center.

9. Osur, *Blacks in the Air Forces*, pp. 57–59.

10. "History of the 477th Bombardment Group," Jan. 15 to July 15, 1949, pp. 1–10; July 16 to Oct. 15, 1944, pp. 28–32.
11. Watson, Mar. 15, 1981.
12. Gropman-James interview.
13. Ibid.; Osur, *Blacks in the Air Forces,* pp. 109–16. For a discussion of other racial incidents in the armed forces in World War II, see Walter White, *A Rising Wind* (Westport, Conn., 1945).
14. Watson, Mar. 15, 1981.
15. Coleman Young to author, Nov. 13, 1980; James Scrapbooks, vol. 6.
16. Major Alan Osur's interview with Colonel Spann Watson, Apr. 3, 1973, Air Force Oral History Program, Simpson Research Center.
17. Gropman, *Air Force Integrates,* p. 29.
18. Osur, *Blacks in the Air Forces,* pp. 118–21.
19. Ibid., p. 200, n. 40.
20. Lieutenant General Benjamin O. Davis, Jr., to author, Oct. 16, 1980.
21. Osur-Watson interview.
22. Author's interview with William Phears, Nov. 30, 1980.
23. *Pittsburgh Courier,* Aug. 30, 1947, p. 5.
24. Osur-Watson interview.
25. Gropman, *Air Force Integrates,* p. 78.
26. "History of 301st Fighter Squadron," July 1, 1948, to Sept. 30, 1948, Group Records, Simpson Research Center.
27. Watson, Mar. 15, 1981.
28. Cox, Oct. 9, 1980.

29. Walter Lewis to Colonel Daniel James, Jr., Jan. 13, 1970 (in author's possession). See also author's interviews with Tuskegee Airmen Fitzroy Newsome, Oct. 17, 1981; Louis R. Purnell, Nov. 17, 1980; Walker, Dec. 15, 1980; and Watson, Mar. 15, 1981.
30. Gropman-James interview.
31. Information for the years at Lockbourne was provided by Davis to author, Oct. 16, 1980, and in author's interviews with James's fellow officers Newsome, Purnell, Walker, and Watson.
32. Walker, Mar. 7, 1981.
33. Richardson, Mar. 4, 1981. Richardson performed in these programs and later in "Operation Happiness."
34. Anderson, June 30, 1980.
35. Charles C. Diggs, Jr., to author, Oct. 20, 1980; Ray Cron to author, Dec. 1, 1980. (Lieutenant Cron was a pilot who flew with James's entourage in "Operation Happiness.")
36. On mink ranch incident see James Scrapbooks, vol. 12.
37. Lieutenant Colonel Jack Marr, a staff officer in Air Force Personnel, began to investigate the effects of segregation in 1948. He called for integration, as did Lieutenant General Idwal H. Edwards, the air force deputy chief of staff for personnel, even before President Truman's order. Gropman, *Air Force Integrates,* pp. 86–91.
38. Paul I. Wellman, *Stuart Symington* (Garden City, 1960), pp. 107–09.
39. Eugene Zuckert to un-

known interviewer, April 1973,
Air Force Oral History Program,
Simpson Research Center.
40. Gropman, *Air Force Integrates,* p. 92.
41. Gropman-James interview.
42. Watson, Mar. 15, 1981.
43. Gropman, *Air Force Integrates,* p. 93; Gropman-James interview.
44. Gropman, *Air Force Integrates,* p. 93; Gropman-James interview. Colonel Spann Watson (ret.), a black flier conversant with this period, estimates that fewer than twenty blacks were flying after the closing of Lockbourne. Because some of them were in bombers, it seems reasonable to assume that about twelve survived in fighters, a number James describes as accurate for blacks flying fighters in Korea. Watson, Mar. 15, 1981. See also Campbell, Apr. 10, 1983.
45. Campbell, Apr. 10, 1983. Colonel Campbell was one of the twelve black officers of staff rank in the air force in 1949 when Lockbourne closed. He described how each of the twelve was sent to schools or staff positions.

Chapter 4

1. Author's interview with Colonel Harry Moreland (ret.), Nov. 15, 1980. Colonel Moreland was operations officer with the Twelfth Fighter-Bomber Squadron in the Eighteenth Fighter Group at Clark Air Force Base. Colonel Howard C. "Scrappy" Johnson

(ret.) to author, Jan. 21, 1981. Johnson was a close friend of Lieutenant James.
2. Gropman-James interview.
3. Moreland, Nov. 15, 1980.
4. Author's interview with Colonel Frank Buzze, Dec. 13, 1980. Buzze was in the same squadron as James.
5. "History of 18th Fighter Group," January to December 1949. Group Records, Simpson Research Center.
6. H. C. Johnson, Jan. 21, 1981.
7. Moreland, Nov. 15, 1980.
8. H. C. Johnson, Jan. 21, 1981.
9. Gropman-James interview.
10. D. W. James, Sept. 3, 1980.
11. George C. Bales to author, Nov. 26, 1980. Bales was an administrative officer with the Eighteenth Fighter Group. He read the reports on the crash.
12. "History of 18th Fighter Group," July to October 1950.
13. Author's interviews with Colonel Robert Dow (ret.), Feb. 6, 1981, and Apr. 18, 1981. Colonel Dow was commanding officer of the Twelfth Fighter-Bomber Squadron in Korea, beginning Aug. 1, 1950.
14. Dean Acheson had defined the U.S. defense perimeter in the Far East excluding South Korea in February 1950. Douglas MacArthur had sounded the same theme in March 1949. William Manchester, *American Caesar: Douglas MacArthur, 1880–1964* (Boston, 1978), pp. 539–40. John W. Spanier in *The Truman-Mac-*

Arthur Controversy and the Korean War (New York, 1964), pp. 25–29, emphasizes the role of John Foster Dulles and his pledges to the South Korean government regarding U.S. protection, the effects of the communist victory in China, and Truman's application of toughness against communism worldwide as bolstering American resolve.
15. Manchester, *American Caesar,* p. 538; Harry J. Middleton, *The Compact History of the Korean War* (New York, 1965), pp. 36–58.
16. Robert Jackson, *Air War over Korea* (New York, 1973), p. 29.
17. "An Evaluation of the Effectiveness of the U.S.A.F. in Korean Campaign: Operations and Tactics," 7 vols., Simpson Research Center, 3:28; Dow, Feb. 6, 1981.
18. Moreland, Dec. 7, 1980.
19. Author's interview with Colonel Daniel Farr (ret.), Jan. 7, 1981. Colonel Farr was a member of the Eighteenth Fighter Group and of James's squadron in Korea. Dow, Feb. 6, 1981. Colonel Dow commanded the Eighteenth Fighter Group.
20. Robert F. Futrell, *The United States Air Force in Korea, 1950–1953* (New York, 1961), p. 163.
21. H. C. Johnson, Jan. 21, 1981.
22. Author's interview with Major Theodore Baader (ret.), Dec. 4, 1980.
23. H. C. Johnson, Jan. 21, 1981.

24. Air Force Reference Branch, National Personnel Records Center, St. Louis, Missouri.
25. "History of 12th Fighter-Bomber Squadron," Oct. 1–31, 1950, Group Records, Simpson Research Center. Dow, Feb. 6, 1981. Colonel Dow was then the commander of the Twelfth Fighter-Bomber Squadron.
26. Accounts of the downing of Lieutenant Claude "Spud" Taylor and of his death are described by Farr, Jan. 7, 1981; H. C. Johnson, Jan. 21, 1981; and Dow, Feb. 6, 1981.
27. Dow, Feb. 6, 1981. For description of Captain James flying "dangerous missions" over North Korea in a reconnaissance jet in January 1951, see *Pittsburgh Courier,* Jan. 27, 1951.
28. Gropman-James interview.

Chapter 5

1. James Biography. See also USAF biographies of Benjamin O. Davis, Jr., William Earl Brown, Jr., Alonzo L. Ferguson, Thomas E. Clifford, and James T. Boddie, Jr. (Simpson Research Center), all black fighter pilot generals at the time of General James's death. Additional information was supplied by the USAF Historical Service on dates or promotion of the above generals.
2. "History of 437th Fighter-Interceptor Squadron," Jan. 1, 1953, to August 1955, Squadron Records, Simpson Research Center; Bertram W. Wilson to author,

Oct. 9, 1980. Wilson was one of the three black pilots at Otis; he describes Chappie in this period as a "born leader." See also Mary Elizabeth Vroman and Nelle Keys Perry, "Demonstrated Ability," *Ladies' Home Journal* 74 (February 1958): 149–52, 154–57.

3. Vroman and Perry, "Demonstrated Ability."

4. Author's interview with Colonel Dennis Sharon (ret.), Oct. 23, 1980. Much information on the RAF Bentwaters period comes from the author's interviews with Sharon and other fliers who served at the time with Lieutenant Colonel James. These interviews include Brigadier General William Kirk, Aug. 25, 1980; Colonel William A. McAdoo, Oct. 15, 1980, and Feb. 9, 1981; Major General Ralph Maglione (ret.), Aug. 25, 1980, and Dec. 12, 1980; Colonel Ed Orr (ret.), Feb. 20, 1981; Colonel Edward Rischer (ret.), Oct. 26, 1980; Colonel Don Henningsen (ret.), Feb. 20, 1983. Also see "History of 81st Fighter Wing," January to June 1962, Wing Records, Simpson Research Center.

5. Charles C. Moskos, "Racial Integration in the Armed Forces," *American Journal of Sociology* 72 (1966): 132–48.

6. Peter Greenberg's interview with General Daniel James, Jr., Dec. 22, 1975, on tape at Tuskegee Institute Archives; Watson, Mar. 15, 1981.

7. *Los Angeles Times,* Opinion section, Jan. 25, 1970, p. 1-F; Watson, Mar. 15, 1981.

8. D. W. James, Sept. 9, 1980.

9. Cox, Mar. 15, 1981.

10. James Biography; author's interview with Gerry Cardozzo, Apr. 18, 1981.

11. Cardozzo, Apr. 18, 1981.

12. Ibid.; Diggs to author, Oct. 20, 1980.

13. Maglione comments, Aug. 25, 1980, led the author to infer James's views on these issues.

14. Henningsen, Feb. 20, 1983.

15. Maglione, Aug. 25, 1980.

16. USAF Biography, Brigadier General Robin Olds, Simpson Research Center.

17. Sharon, Oct. 23, 1980.

18. Kirk, Aug. 25, 1980.

19. Maglione, Aug. 25, 1980.

20. Orr, Feb. 20, 1980.

21. Author's interview with Colonel William J. Baugh, Jan. 18, 1981.

22. Rischer, Dec. 12, 1980.

23. Kirk, Aug. 25, 1980.

24. Author's interviews with Colonel David Swennes and Colonel Clark Price, Aug. 25, 1980; Sharon, Oct. 23, 1980.

25. Maglione, Aug. 25, 1980.

26. Kirk, Aug. 25, 1980.

27. Ibid.

28. Rischer, Oct. 26, 1980.

29. Henningsen, Feb. 20, 1983.

30. Maglione, Jan. 12, 1981.

31. McAdoo, Oct. 15, 1980.

32. Orr, Aug. 25, 1981.

33. Author's interview with air force officer who requested anonymity.

34. Greenberg-James interview.

35. Orr, Feb. 20, 1981.

36. General Daniel James, Jr., Martin L. King Memorial Speech, Jan. 15, 1976, on tape at

Tuskegee Institute Archives.
37. Orr, May 1, 1981.
38. Price, June 8, 1983.
39. Frazier, July 14, 1981;
Kirk, Aug. 25, 1980; Orr, May 1,
1981.
40. Greenberg-James interview;
Orr, May 1, 1981.

Chapter 6

1. Robert F. Futrell, "The Situation," in *Aces and Aerial Victories: The United States Air Force in Southeast Asia, 1965–1973,* ed. James N. Eastman, Jr., Walter Hank, and Lawrence J. Paszek (Montgomery, 1976), pp. 1–17. See also McAdoo, Nov. 12, 1980.
2. "History of the 8th Tactical Fighter Wing," July 1966 to December 1966, Group Records, Simpson Research Center, pp. 19–24, 27. The Eighth Tactical Fighter Wing averaged 162.4 sorties per aircraft between July and December 1966.
3. McAdoo, Nov. 12, 1980; author's interview with Colonel Everett T. Raspberry (ret.), May 4, 1981.
4. Eastman, Hank, and Paszek, *Aces and Aerial Victories,* pp. 39–40.
5. Author's interview with Ruby Gilmore, October 7, 1980. Ms. Gilmore was a civilian employed by the Defense Department as Robin Olds's secretary at Bentwaters and Ubon.
6. Kirk, Aug. 25, 1980.
7. See Carolyn Dubose,

"Chappie James," *Ebony* 25 (October 1970): 153, for quote of James's motto. Colonel William A. McAdoo remembered James using it in Vietnam (McAdoo, Nov. 12, 1980).
8. McAdoo, Nov. 12, 1980.
9. Ibid.
10. Kirk, Aug. 25, 1980.
11. Colonel Thomas C. Wilkinson to author, Nov. 26, 1980.
12. Orr, May 1, 1981.
13. Project CHECO Reports, Southeast Asia Special Report, "Air-to-Air Encounters over North Vietnam, January 1, 1967–June 30, 1967," 3 vols., classified secret, Simpson Research Center, 1:6, 8, 9, 11, 42.
14. Ibid., 1:10.
15. Raspberry, May 4, 1981.
16. Ibid.
17. *Seventh Air Force News,* Jan. 6, 1967, Simpson Research Center, pp. 1, 15; and Colonel Robin Olds interview, n.d., 1967, Simpson Research Center, p. 1. See also Eastman, Hank, and Paszek, *Aces and Aerial Victories,* pp. 38–40.
18. Raspberry, May 4, 1981.
19. Eastman, Hank, and Paszek, *Aces and Aerial Victories,* p. 40.
20. See Greenberg-James interview.
21. Author's interview with Lieutenant Colonel Earl J. Barnhill, Nov. 13, 1980.
22. Citation accompanying the award of the Legion of Merit (in author's possession).
23. *New York Times,* Aug. 11, 1967, p. 3. On later militancy

among black soldiers in Vietnam, however, see Wallace Terry, "Black Power in Vietnam," *Time* 94 (Sept. 19, 1969): 22–23.

24. Peter Braestrup to author, Oct. 17, 1980.

25. U.S., Congress, Senate, *Congressional Record,* 90th Cong., 2d sess., 1968, 114, 6514.

26. Chief Master Sergeant Byron D. Straus to Colonel James, Jan. 5, 1970 (in author's possession).

27. Olds Biography, p. 3.

28. Kirk, Aug. 25, 1980.

29. *Philadelphia Inquirer,* Jan. 7, 1968, p. 7-F, and *Washington Post,* Dec. 14, 1967, p. 6-A.

30. Lyndon B. Johnson to Colonel Daniel James, Jr., Feb. 26, 1968 (copy in author's possession), and Colonel Daniel James, Jr., to President Lyndon B. Johnson, Mar. 5, 1968 (copy in author's possession).

Chapter 7

1. Kirk, Aug. 25, 1980.

2. D. W. James, May 19, 1981.

3. Daniel James, Jr., to L. Mendel Rivers, Feb. 5, 1969 (copy in author's possession).

4. L. Mendel Rivers to Charles C. Diggs, Jr., Jan. 16, 1969, and Bob Sikes to Charles C. Diggs, Jr., Jan. 16, 1969 (copy of each in author's possession).

5. James to Rivers, June 12, 1968 (copy in author's possession). See also Rivers to James, May 29, 1968 (copy in author's possession), in which Rivers

sends pictures of their meeting.

6. Author's interview with Robert Sikes, Aug. 15, 1980.

7. Colonel Daniel James, Jr., to the Honorable Bob Sikes, Jan. 19, 1968 (copy in author's possession).

8. James to Rivers, June 12, 1968; James to Sikes, Mar. 25, 1968.

9. Sikes, Aug. 15, 1980.

10. Ibid.

11. Speaking itinerary of Colonel Daniel James, Jr., culled from notes of his secretary, Julie McCaulay (notes in author's possession).

12. Ibid. See also Colonel Franklin L. Fisher's nomination of Colonel James for Waterman Award, Sept. 11, 1968 (copy in author's possession), and *Trumbull Times,* July 9, 1970, for description of James as honorary marshall of Barnum Day Festival in Bridgeport, Connecticut, in James Scrapbooks, vol. 2; and see conferral of Horatio Alger Award on James, in James Scrapbooks, vol. 3.

13. Colonel Daniel James, Jr., to Dr. Gary F. Sowers, June 17, 1969 (copy in author's possession).

14. Russell J. Hart to President Lyndon B. Johnson, Mar. 18, 1968 (copy in author's possession).

15. W. E. Morgan to General William Momyer, Mar. 3, 1969 (copy in author's possession).

16. Margaret E. Jones to Mr. (Jim) Conway, Mar. 6, 1969 (copy in author's possession).

17. Mary Schreiber to Mr. (Jim) Conway, Mar. 5, 1969 (copy in author's possession).
18. Ted I. Honey to Colonel Daniel James, Jr., July 10, 1968 (copy in author's possession).
19. J. Allen Ball to Colonel Daniel James, Jan. 29, 1968 (copy in author's possession).
20. Kirk, Aug. 25, 1980.
21. C. George, Jan. 18, 1981.
22. *Los Angeles Times,* Jan. 25, 1970.
23. Author's interview with Julie McCaulay, July 14, 1980.
24. Colonel Daniel James, Jr., to Colonel Max Rogers, July 30, 1968 (copy in author's possession).
25. McCaulay, July 14, 1980.
26. Colonel Daniel James, Jr., to Brigadier General E. B. Edwards, Mar. 10, 1969 (copy in author's possession).
27. Robert C. Seamans, Jr., to author, Nov. 19, 1980.

Chapter 8

1. The classic discussion of Wheelus and the relations of the Libyan and American governments concerning that base and leading to the American withdrawal is contained in a multivolume study classified as secret, James Spiros, "History of the USAF Withdrawal from Libya: The Closure of Wheelus Air Force Base and the Inactivation of the 7272d Flying Training Wing," 10 vols., Simpson Research Center, 1971, 1:1–17.
2. Information on the "box incident" and its repercussions may be found in an interview by *New York Times* reporters Tom Johnson and Roger Wilkens with General Daniel James, Jr., March 1976, on tape at Tuskegee Institute Archives.
3. Spiros, "Withdrawal from Libya," 1:25; Johnson-Wilkens-James interview.
4. Spiros, "Withdrawal from Libya," vol. 5, document 2.
5. Ibid., after document 12, "The Future of Wheelus."
6. Sikes, Aug. 15, 1980.
7. *Pittsburgh Press,* Jan. 19, 1978, p. 5-A. Melvin Laird, secretary of defense at that time, confirmed this story in an interview with the author, Nov. 6, 1980.
8. Spiros, "Withdrawal from Libya," 1:33; ibid., vol. 6, document 95, American Embassy, Tripoli, to Secretary of State, Oct. 23, 1969.
9. Ibid., 1:38–45.
10. Ibid., 1:39–45.
11. Ibid., 1:49–63.
12. Congressman Bill Nichols to author, Sept. 24, 1980.
13. Laird, Nov. 6, 1980.
14. Spiros, "Withdrawal from Libya," 1:1–3.
15. Air Force News Service, Feb. 7, 1970, feature no. 2-27-53F.
16. Author's interview with Dan Henkin, Aug. 23, 1980; Laird, Nov. 6, 1980.
17. Seamans to author, Nov. 19, 1980.
18. Laird, Nov. 6, 1980.
19. Cox, Mar. 8, 1983; Watson,

Feb. 28, 1983. Cox and Watson were colonels who had an intimate knowledge of the views of Tuskegee Airmen on James's appointment as general. Author's interviews with former air force colonels and Tuskegee Airmen William Campbell, Apr. 10, 1983; Charles Cooper, Apr. 25, 1983; and Charles McGee, Apr. 26, 1983.

20. Price, Feb. 18, 1983; author's interviews with Brigadier General James T. Boddie, Jr., Feb. 18, 1983. See also USAF biographies of Benjamin O. Davis, Jr., James T. Boddie, Jr., Alonzo L. Ferguson, Thomas E. Clifford, and William Earl Brown, Jr. (Simpson Research Center), all generals and fighter pilots.

21. Colonel Daniel James, Jr., to Thomas Burnett, Registrar, Tuskegee Institute, May 15, 1969 (copy in author's possession).

22. *New York Times*, Jan. 26, 1970, p. 13.

23. Ibid.

24. Bob Sikes to Colonel Daniel James, Jr., Jan. 1, 1970 (copy in author's possession).

25. Major Denny Sharon to Colonel Daniel James, Jr., Dec. 29, 1969 (copy in author's possession).

26. Billy Patton to Colonel Daniel James, Jr., Dec. 31, 1969 (copy in author's possession).

27. H. Wynne to Colonel Daniel James, Jr., Jan. 3, 1970 (copy in author's possession).

28. Dick Collins to Colonel Daniel James, Jr., Jan. 4, 1970 (copy in author's possession).

29. Father Tom Heffernan to Colonel Daniel James, Jr., Jan. 10, 1970 (copy in author's possession).

30. Sergeant George T. Bedell to Colonel Daniel James, Jr., Dec. 31, 1969 (copy in author's possession).

31. Brigadier General Robin Olds to Colonel Daniel James, Jr., Jan. 5, 1969 (copy in author's possession).

32. General H. M. Wade to Colonel Daniel James, Jr., Jan. 8, 1970 (copy in author's possession).

33. *Washington Post*, Feb. 1, 1970.

Chapter 9

1. A useful summary of literate opinion on the "fall of Vietnam" that is also applicable to the early 1970s is in Earl Ravenal, "The Consequences of the End Game in Vietnam," *Foreign Affairs* 53 (July 1975): 651–67.

2. Henry Kissinger, *White House Years* (Boston, 1979), pp. 227–28.

3. This assessment of the problems facing the Department of Defense is derived from the author's conversations with Melvin Laird, Nov. 6, 1980, and with Dan Henkin and Jerry Freidheim, Dec. 28, 1981. Freidheim was principal deputy to Henkin in 1970 and succeeded in 1972 to the post of assistant secretary of defense for public affairs.

4. *Manchester Union-Leader,* May 24, 1971, in James Scrapbooks, vol. 8.

5. Freidheim, Dec. 28, 1981.

6. Author's interview with Fred Hoffman, Feb. 13, 1981, and phone interview with Bob Schieffer, Mar. 17, 1981.

7. Most observations on James while at the Pentagon are from Dan Henkin and Jerry Freidheim, his immediate superiors. Secretary Laird also has contributed useful observations as has Captain Larry Hamilton, a navy commander during General James's Pentagon years and an executive assistant to James. See author's interview with Captain Larry Hamilton, Feb. 27, 1981. See also author's interview with Jo Valente, Oct. 30, 1980. Ms. Valente was General James's secretary while at the Defense Department.

8. *Bristol Press,* Nov. 27, 1970 (in Zubkoff Files, the Pentagon); *Chicago Tribune,* Sept. 27, 1970; H. Ross Perot to author, Jan. 15, 1981.

9. *Pittsburgh Press,* Jan. 19, 1978, p. 5-A.

10. Henry S. Blank to Brigadier General Daniel James, Jr., May 14, 1970 (copy in author's possession; see also copy in James Scrapbooks, vol. 1). See also *Pensacola News Journal,* Feb. 27, 1978, p. 7.

11. Interview of correspondent from *Jet* magazine with General Daniel James, Jr., Mar. 30, 1976, on tape at Tuskegee Institute Archives.

12. *Fond du Lac Commonwealth-Reporter,* Jan. 19, 1971 (Zubkoff Files). For copies of most Wisconsin newspapers concerning the incident, see James Scrapbooks, vol. 5.

13. *Sheboygan Press,* Jan. 28, 1971, p. 1.

14. *Jet*-James interview.

15. *Wisconsin State Journal,* Jan. 28, 1971, p. 1.

16. Ibid.

17. *Jet*-James interview.

18. Ibid.

19. Perot to author, Jan. 15, 1981.

20. Author's interview with Curt Smothers, Sept. 1, 1980. Smothers was General James's lawyer and a former air force officer; see *Ebony* 26 (April 1971): 36 and *Ebony* 29 (May 1974): 91.

21. Author's interview with Johnny Ford, Sept. 17, 1980.

22. Sammy Davis, Jr., and Company, WRC-TV, May 16, 1976, on tape at Tuskegee Institute Archives.

23. Bobbie J. Griffin to General Daniel James, Jr., Jan. 1, 1970 (copy in author's possession).

24. *Chicago Tribune,* Sept. 27, 1970. Senator Barry Goldwater to author, Oct. 10, 1980, describes James's talk to black cadets.

25. *Pensacola News Journal,* Mar. 27, 1978, p. 1.

26. "General Daniel James, Jr.," *Kappa Alpha Psi Journal* 57 (May 1971): 70, in James Scrapbooks, vol. 20.

27. Text of Phil Donahue show with General James, June 4,

1971, in James Scrapbooks, vol. 8.

28. Moore, June 30, 1980. See James's comments ("These young black people suffering all these obstacles to equality. Bull! Most of these obstacles are illusionary") in the *Washington Post,* July 21, 1975, p. 16-A.

29. Johnson-Wilkens-James interview.

30. U.S. Congress, House, *Congressional Record,* 91st Cong. 2d sess., 1970, 5842. Information on criticism of James from blacks in Pensacola came from his sister, Lillie James Frazier, Feb. 12, 1981.

31. Bulletin, Department of State, *Continuing U.S. Efforts on Behalf of Prisoners of War and Missing in Southeast Asia,* vol. 65, no. 1687, Oct. 25, 1971, pp. 447–50.

32. Author's interview with Colonel William M. Taylor, Sept. 4, 1980. Colonel Taylor attended the same dinner as a military assistant to the secretary of defense.

33. Author's interview with Iris Powers, Feb. 1, 1981. Mrs. Powers was a prominent early leader in the National League of Families.

34. U.S. Congress, House, Committee on Foreign Affairs, Hearings before the Subcommittee on National Security Policy and Scientific Developments, *American Prisoners of War in Southeast Asia, 1971,* 92d Cong., pt. 2, app., pp. 157, 163.

35. Author's interview with Charles Havens, Dec. 28, 1980.

Havens was a lawyer who worked with the National League of Families and often worked with General James.

36. Jerry Freidheim to author, Oct. 31, 1980.

37. Author's interview with Joan Vincent, Jan. 17, 1981. Mrs. Vincent is a past president of the league.

38. Bob Hope to author, Mar. 12, 1981.

39. Richard M. Nixon to author, May 18, 1981.

40. Freidheim to author, Oct. 31, 1980.

41. General James's speech before Horatio Alger Award Committee, June 1976, on tape at Tuskegee Institute Archives. Dr. Norman Vincent Peale made the presentation to James. The Horatio Alger Award is given annually to Americans who have demonstrated unusual initiative and personal accomplishment.

42. *Baltimore Sun,* Apr. 24, 1973, p. 15.

43. Henkin and Freidheim, Dec. 28, 1981. For praise of James's work, see also Melvin Laird to Dan Henkin (copy) and Melvin Laird to General Daniel James, Jr., Nov. 10, 1970, in James Scrapbooks, vol. 3.

44. Author's interview with John McLucas, Feb. 12, 1981.

45. Freidheim to author, Oct. 31, 1980.

46. McLucas, Feb. 12, 1981.

47. Author's interview with General P. K. Carlton, Dec. 15, 1980.

48. William P. Clements to author, Mar. 20, 1981.

49. Anonymous colleague of General James, in Office of Assistant Secretary of Defense for Public Affairs, to author, Dec. 8, 1981.

50. D. W. James, Sept. 3, 1980.

Chapter 10

1. *Wall Street Journal,* Nov. 27, 1976, p. 2-F.

2. NORAD, fact sheet, "NORAD Cheyenne Mountain Complex," pp. 1–9; "The North American Air Defense Command," pp. 1–22.

3. *Wall Street Journal,* Nov. 27, 1976, p. 2-F.

4. Swennes, July 1, 1981. Colonel Swennes was General James's aide at Scott Air Force Base and executive officer at NORAD.

5. General William K. Carr to author, Apr. 27, 1981; General Carr's remarks at General James's farewell party at Peterson Air Force Base, on tape at Tuskegee Institute Archives.

6. Carr to author, Apr. 27, 1981.

7. *Kansas City Star,* July 16, 1975, p. 5.

8. Rose Elder recalls hearing General James complain to former President Ford about Carter's decision on the B-1 (author's interview with Rose Elder, July 2, 1981).

9. Ned Scharff's interview with General Daniel James, Jr., Apr. 28, 1976, on tape at Tuskegee Institute Archives.

10. Sammy Davis, Jr., and Company, WRC-TV, May 16, 1976.

11. General James's address to Doolittle Chapter of the Air Force Association, Mar. 5, 1976, on tape at Tuskegee Institute Archives.

12. D. W. James, June 28, 1981; Swennes, July 1, 1981.

13. For details of controversies involved in the reorganization of NORAD see *Colorado Springs Sun,* Jan. 26, 1978; author's interview with an air force colonel privy to discussions between General James and General Jones who asked that his name not be identified. See also *Washington Post,* Nov. 23, 1977, p. 17; Price, July 1, 1981; and author's interview with Colonel Cato Reeves, Mar. 17, 1981.

14. Author's interview with Colonel Art Ragan, Mar. 15, 1981.

15. Swennes, July 1, 1981.

16. "Chappie" to Bill Baker, Oct. 20, 1977 (copy in author's possession).

17. Swennes, July 1, 1981.

18. Price, July 1, 1981.

19. *Colorado Springs Sun,* Jan. 26, 1978.

20. Author's interview with Jerry Pate, May 15, 1978.

21. Author's interview with General James's lawyer Curt Smothers, Sept. 1, 1980. Southern Railroad had offered General James a position on its board; the G. D. Searle Company also reportedly was negotiating with

him. On First Artists film, see the *Hollywood Reporter,* Apr. 13, 1978, p. 10. Author's interview with General James's close friend in Pensacola, insurance man Dave Johnson, Aug. 10, 1980. *New York Times,* Feb. 26, 1978. Reeves (James's aide), Feb. 26, 1981.

22. *Washington Post,* Feb. 26, 1978.

23. Reeves, Feb. 26, 1981.

24. Retirement ceremony for General Daniel James, Jr., Jan. 26, 1978, Pentagon press release (Zubkoff Files).

25. Christmas card, 1977, Chappie and Dottie James to Mrs. John Long. The former describe their last Christmas in "their beloved Air Force."

26. Script, WRC-TV, Jan. 26, 1978 (Zubkoff Files). Lillie James Frazier, Aug. 20, 1981, described the subdued tone of her brother's voice when he first mentioned his mother.

27. *Washington Post,* Mar. 1, 1978.

28. Television interview with General James, WTTG-TV, Feb. 13, 1978 (Zubkoff Files).

29. Elder, July 2, 1981.

30. D. W. James, June 28, 1981.

31. Price, July 1, 1981; Swennes, July 1, 1981.

32. *Colorado Springs Gazette Telegraph,* Feb. 26, 1978, p. 1.

33. D. W. James, June 28, 1981.

34. Elder, July 2, 1981.

35. Smothers, Sept. 1, 1980.

36. Henkin, Dec. 28, 1981.

37. *Pensacola Journal,* Mar. 2, 1978, p. 1; Mar. 3, 1978, pp. 1, 10.

38. *Richmond Afro-American and Planet,* Mar. 11, 1978.

39. *Washington Post,* Mar. 2, 1978.

40. *Indianapolis Star,* Mar. 6, 1978.

41. *Air Force Times,* Mar. 20, 1978.

42. *Los Angeles Times,* Feb. 26, 1978.

Chapter 11

1. United States Air Force, "Report to the United States Air Force Equal Opportunity Conference," 2 vols. (October 1971), 2:278–82.

2. Walter A. Collins, "The Race Problem in the United States Air Force" (Thesis, Air Command and Staff College, Air University, Maxwell Air Force Base, 1972), p. 33.

3. J. Ford, Sept. 17, 1980.

4. Smothers, Sept. 1, 1980.

5. Reeves, Feb. 26, 1981.

6. *Colorado Springs Gazette Telegraph,* Feb. 26, 1978, in James Scrapbooks, vol. 37.

7. Ragan, Apr. 25, 1981.

8. Pat Sampson's interview with General Daniel James, Jr., July 19, 1976, on tape at Tuskegee Institute Archives.

9. General James's speech, Oklahoma Football Banquet, Jan. 31, 1976, p. 3 (copy at Office of Athletic Director, Oklahoma University).

10. *Proceedings of the Eighty-Second Continental Congress, National Society of the Daughters of the American Revolution,* Washington, D.C., Apr. 16–19, 1973, p. 20.

11. Ted Stewart, "In praise of the New Jesse," *Sepia* 24 (August 1975): 82.

12. Press conference, Scott Air Force Base, July 7, 1975, on tape at Tuskegee Institute Archives; General James's speech to Pike's Peak Council of Boy Scouts of America, Nov. 24, 1975, on tape at Tuskegee Institute Archives.

13. Oklahoma Football Banquet speech, p. 3.

14. General James Day in Pensacola occurred Sept. 16, 1975.

15. General James's address to Officers Wives Club luncheon, Jan. 13, 1976, on tape at Tuskegee Institute Archives.

16. General James's address to Links Organization, March 1976, on tape at Tuskegee Institute Archives.

17. *Kansas City Star,* Mar. 19, 1972; Sampson-James interview; Clements to author, Mar. 20, 1981.

Bibliography

Books

Dalfiume, Richard M. *Desegregation of the U.S. Armed Forces: Fighting on Two Fronts, 1939–1953*. Columbia, Mo.: University of Missouri Press, 1969.

Eastman, James N., Jr.; Hank, Walter; and Paszek, Lawrence J., eds. *Aces and Aerial Victories: The United States Air Force in Southeast Asia, 1965–1973*. Montgomery, Ala.: Albert F. Simpson Historical Research Center, 1976.

Factor, Robert L. *The Black Response to America*. Reading, Mass.: Addison Wesley, 1970.

Foner, Jack D. *Blacks and the Military in American History: A New Perspective*. New York: Praeger, 1974.

Francis, Charles E. *The Tuskegee Airmen: The Story of the Negro in the U.S. Air Force*. Boston: Bruce Humphries, 1955.

Futrell, Robert F. *The United States Air Force in Korea, 1950–1953*. New York: Duell, Sloan and Pearce, 1961.

———. *The United States Air Force in Southeast Asia: The Advisory Years to 1965*. Washington, D.C.: Office of Air Force History, 1981.

Gropman, Alan L. *The Air Force Integrates 1945–1964*. Washington, D.C.: Office of Air Force History, 1978.

Harlan, Louis R. *Booker T. Washington: The Making of a Black Leader, 1856–1901*. New York: Oxford, 1972.

———. *Booker T. Washington, Wizard of Tuskegee, 1901–1915*. New York: Oxford, 1983.

Hastie, William H. *On Clipped Wings: The Story of Jim Crow in the Army Air Corps*. Washington, D.C.: NAACP, 1943.

Jackson, Robert. *Air War over Korea*. New York: Scribners, 1973.

Johnson, Charles S. *Growing Up in the Black Belt: Negro Youth in the Rural South*. Washington: American Council on Education, 1941.

Kissinger, Henry. *White House Years*. Boston: Little, Brown, 1979.

MacGregor, Morris J., Jr. *Integration of the Armed Forces 1940–1965*. Washington, D.C.: Center of Military History, 1981.

Manchester, William. *American Caesar: Douglas MacArthur, 1880–1964*. Boston: Little, Brown, 1978.

Middleton, Harry J. *The Compact History of the Korean War*. New York: Hawthorne, 1965.

Mullen, Robert W. *Blacks in America's Wars: The Shift in Attitudes from the Revolutionary War to Vietnam*. New York: Monad Press, 1973.

Murray, Pauli. *States' Law on Race and Color*. Cincinnati: Woman's Division of Christian Service, Board of Missions and Church Extension, Methodist Church, 1951.

Osur, Alan M. *Blacks in the Army Air Forces During World War II: The Problem of Race Relations*. Washington, D.C.: Office of Air Force History, 1977.

Rose, Robert A. *Lonely Eagles*. Los Angeles: n.p., 1976.

Rosengarten, Theodore. *All God's Dangers: The Life of Nate Shaw*. New York: Knopf, 1975.

Spanier, John W. *The Truman-MacArthur Controversy and the Korean War*. New York: W. W. Norton, 1964.

Stillman, Richard J. *Integration of the Negro in the U.S. Armed Forces*. New York: Praeger, 1968.

Washington, Booker T. *The Negro in Business*. Boston: Hertel, Jenkins, 1907.

Wellman, Paul I. *Stuart Symington*. Garden City: Doubleday, 1960.

White, Walter. *A Rising Wind*. Westport, Conn.: Negro University Press, 1945.

Wright, Richard. *Black Boy: A Record of Childhood and Youth*. 1945. Reprint. New York: Harper and Row, 1945.

Unpublished Studies

Collins, Walter A. "The Race Problem in the United States Air Force." Thesis, Air Command and Staff College, Air University, Maxwell Air Force Base, Montgomery, Ala., 1972.

Miscellaneous

Butler, Thomas B. "Four Stars Flying." *Floridian,* magazine for *St. Petersberg Times,* January 18, 1976.

General James Scrapbooks. Tuskegee Institute Archives. 37 vols.

Proceedings of the Eighty-Second Continental Congress, National Society of the Daughters of the American Revolution. Washington, D.C. April 16–19, 1973.

United States Air Force. "Report to the United States Air Force Equal

Opportunity Conference." 2 vols. Maxwell Air Force Base, Montgomery, Ala., October 1971.

Articles and Pamphlets

Bragaw, Donald M. "Status of Negroes in a Southern Port City in the Progressive Era: Pensacola, 1896–1920." *Florida Historical Quarterly* 51 (January 1973):281–302.

————. "Loss of Identity in Pensacola's Past: A Creole Footnote." *Florida Historical Quarterly* 50 (April 1972):414–18.

Dubose, Carolyn. "Chappie James, A New Role For An Old Warrior." *Ebony* 25 (October 1970):153–56.

Finkle, Lee. "The Conservative Arms of Militant Rhetoric: Black Protest during World War II." *Journal of American History* 60 (1973):692–713.

"General Daniel James, Jr.: His Story is a Study in Success." *Kappa Alpha Psi Journal* 57 (May 1971):68–71.

Moskos, Charles C. "Racial Integration in the Armed Forces." *American Journal of Sociology* 72 (1966):132–48.

Paszek, Lawrence J. "Separate But Equal." *Aerospace Historian* 24 (September 1977):135–45.

————. "Negroes and the Air Force, 1939–1949." *Military Affairs* 31 (1967):1–9.

Ravenal, Éarl. "The Consequences of the End Game in Vietnam." *Foreign Affairs* 53 (July 1975):651–67.

Terry, Wallace. "Black Power in Vietnam." *Time* 94 (September 19, 1969):22–23.

Vroman, Mary Elizabeth, and Perry, Nelle Keys. "Demonstrated Ability." *Ladies' Home Journal* 74 (February 1958):149–57.

Government Documents

An Act to Authorize the President to Appoint General Omar N. Bradley to the Permanent Rank of General. *Statutes at Large*, 64, A 224 (1950–1951).

Bulletin. Department of State. *Continuing U.S. Efforts on Behalf of Prisoners of War and Missing in Southeast Asia*, 65, No. 1687 (October 25, 1971):447–50.

Fourteenth Census of the United States, 1920, Population, II: Washington, D.C., 1921.

Twelfth Census of the United States, 1900, Population, I: Washington, D.C.: 1901.

190 Bibliography

U.S., Congress, House. Committee on Foreign Affairs. Hearings before the Subcommittee on National Security Policy and Scientific Developments, *American Prisoners of War in Southeast Asia, 1971,* 92d Cong. p. 2, app., pp. 157, 163.
U.S., Congress, House. *Congressional Record,* 91st Cong., 2d sess., 1970, 5842
U.S., Congress, Senate. *Congressional Record,* 90th Cong., 2d sess., 1968, 114, 6514.

Unpublished Duplicated Material

Project CHECO Reports, Southeast Asia Special Report. "Air-to-Air Encounters over North Vietnam, January 1, 1967–June 30, 1967." 3 vols. Typed copy, classified secret. Maxwell Air Force Base, Montgomery, Ala.: Albert F. Simpson Historical Research Center, 1967.
Spiros, James. "History of the USAF Withdrawal from Libya: The Closure of Wheelus Air Force Base and the Inactivation of the 7272d Flying Training Wing." 10 vols. Typed copy, classified secret. Maxwell Air Force Base, Montgomery, Ala.: Albert F. Simpson Historical Research Center, 1971.
Text of Phil Donahue Show with General James, June 4, 1971, in James Scrapbooks, vol. 8, Tuskegee Institute Archives.

Unit Histories and Miscellaneous Studies
(All at Albert F. Simpson Historical Research Center, Maxwell Air Force Base, Montgomery, Ala.)

"An Evaluation of the Effectiveness of the U.S.A.F. in Korean Campaign: Operations and Tactics." 7 vols. Study by U.S.A.F. Evaluation Group headed by Major General Glenn Barcus.
"History of 8th Tactical Fighter Wing." January 1966 to December 1967.
"History of 12th Fighter-Bomber Squadron." July 5 to December 1950.
"History of 18th Fighter Group." January to December 1949, January to December 1950.
"History of 437th Fighter-Interceptor Squadron." Squadron Records. January 1, 1953, to August 1955.
"History of the 477th Bombardment Group (Medium)." January 15, 1944, to July 15, 1949.
"History of the 477th Composite Group." September 15, 1945, to June 30, 1947.
"History of 301st Fighter Squadron." July 1947 to January 1949.
"History of 81st Fighter Wing." January 1961 to December 1963.

Bibliography

Interviews with Author

Charles A. Anderson, June 30, 1980.
Major Theodore Baader, December 4, 1980.
Lieutenant Colonel Earl J. Barnhill, November 13, 1980.
Colonel William J. Baugh, January 18, 1981.
Brigadier General James T. Boddie, Jr., February 18, 1983.
Dr. S. W. Boyd, November 10, 1980.
Muriel Brown, April 17, 1973.
Colonel Frank Buzze, December 13, 1980.
Colonel William Campbell, April 10, 1983.
Gerry Cardozzo, April 18, 1981.
General P. K. Carlton, December 15, 1980.
Colonel Charles Cooper, April 25, 1983.
T. C. Cotrell, June 30, 1980.
Colonel Hannibal Cox, October 9, 1980; March 8, 1981; March 15, 1981; March 22, 1981.
Richard Crenshaw, December 27, 1980.
Marie Davis, January 5, 1981.
Colonel Robert Dow, February 6, 1981; April 18, 1981.
Oscar "Tobey" Downs, October 19, 1980.
Rose Elder, July 2, 1981.
Colonel Daniel Farr, January 7, 1981.
Johnny Ford, September 17, 1980; February 27, 1981.
Lillie James Frazier, August 20, 1980; January 10, 1981; January 12, 1981; January 20, 1981; February 12, 1981; February 20, 1981; July 14, 1981.
Jerry Freidheim, December 28, 1981; October 31, 1980.
Lucille Galry, January 5, 1981.
Claude George, January 18, 1981.
Wilbur George, January 18, 1981.
Ruby Gilmore, October 7, 1980.
Captain Larry Hamilton, February 27, 1981.
Rex Harvey, April 17, 1973.
Charles Havens, December 28, 1980.
Dan Henkin, August 23, 1980; December 28, 1981.
Colonel Don Henningsen, February 20, 1983.
Fred Hoffman, February 13, 1981.
Gloria Hunter, June 10, 1980.
Dorothy Watkins James, September 3, 1980; September 9, 1980; May 19, 1981; June 28, 1981; December 20, 1983.
Maudeste James, January 10, 1981.
Dr. Thomas James, December 15, 1980; March 20, 1981; July 18, 1983.
Dave Johnson, August 10, 1980.
Colonel Howard C. Johnson, January 21, 1981.

Corrine Jones, April 17, 1973.
Brigadier General William Kirk, August 25, 1980.
Melvin Laird, November 6, 1980.
Colonel William A. McAdoo, January 15, 1980; October 15, 1980; November 12, 1980; February 9, 1981.
Julie McCaulay, July 14, 1980.
Vernon McDaniel, January 18, 1981.
Colonel Charles McGee, April 26, 1983.
John McLucas, February 12, 1981.
Gloria McMillan, December 15, 1980.
T. H. McVoy, April 17, 1973.
Major General Ralph Maglione, August 25, 1980; December 19, 1980; January 12, 1981.
Robert Moore, June 30, 1980.
Colonel Harry Moreland, November 15,1980; December 7, 1980; January 15, 1981.
Joe Morris, March 10, 1981.
Fitzroy Newsome, October 17, 1981.
Colonel Ed Orr, February 20, 1981; May 1, 1981; August 25, 1981.
Jerry Pate, May 15, 1978.
William Phears, November 30, 1980.
Iris Powers, February 1, 1981.
Colonel Clark Price, August 25, 1980; July 1, 1981; February 18, 1983; June 8, 1983.
Louis R. Purnell, November 17, 1980.
Colonel Art Ragan, April 25, 1981.
Napoleon Rancifer, April 13, 1973.
Colonel Everett T. Rasberry, May 4, 1981.
Colonel Cato Reeves, February 26, 1981; March 17, 1981.
Walter Richardson, March 4 and 16, 1981.
Colonel Edward Rischer, October 26, 1980; December 12, 1980.
Rosebud Robinson, April 17, 1973.
Bob Schieffer, March 17, 1981.
Colonel Dennis Sharon, October 23, 1980.
Robert Sikes, August 15, 1980.
Curt Smothers, September 1, 1980.
Colonel David Swennes, August 25, 1980; July 1, 1981.
Colonel William M. Taylor, September 4, 1980.
Jo Valente, October 30, 1980.
Joan Vincent, January 17, 1981.
Charles E. Walker, December 15, 1980; March 7, 1981.
Colonel Spann Watson, March 15, 1981; February 28, 1983.
Colonel James T. Wiley, March 11, 1981.
James Woodson, July 1, 1980.

Interviews, Air Force Oral History Program
(Typescripts available at Albert F. Simpson Historical Research Center, Maxwell Air Force Base, Montgomery, Ala.)

Major General Daniel James, Jr., by Major Alan Gropman, October 2, 1973.
Colonel Robin Olds by unknown interviewer, no date, 1967.
Brigadier General Noel F. Parrish by Major Alan Gropman, March 30, 1973.
Colonel Spann Watson by Major Alan Osur, April 3, 1973.
Eugene Zuckert by unknown interviewer, April 1973.

Interviews on Tape at Tuskegee Institute Archives

General Daniel James, Jr., by Peter Greenberg, December 22, 1975.
General Daniel James, Jr., by reporter from *Jet* magazine, March 30, 1976.
General Daniel James Jr., by Tom Johnson and Roger Wilkens, March, 1976.
General Daniel James, Jr., by Pat Sampson, July 19, 1976.
General Daniel James, Jr., by Ned Scharff, April 28, 1976.

Speeches by General James
(On Tape at Tuskegee Institute Archives)

Horatio Alger Society Presentation, June 1976.
"Americanism," May 10, 1976.
Sammy Davis, Jr., and Company, WRC-TV, May 16, 1976.
Doolittle Chapter, Air Force Association, March 5, 1976.
Farewell Party, Peterson Air Force Base, February 1978.
Martin L. King Memorial Speech, January 15, 1976.
Links Organization, March 1976.
Officers Wives Club Luncheon, January 13, 1976.
Pike's Peak Council of Boy Scouts of America, November 24, 1975.
Press Conference, Scott Air Force Base, July 7, 1975.
United Negro College Fund Banquet, October 29, 1976.

Newspapers

Air Force Times　　　　　*Colorado Springs*
Baltimore Sun　　　　　　*Gazette Telegraph*

Colorado Springs Sun
Fond du Lac
  Commonwealth-Reporter
Hollywood Reporter
Indianapolis Star
Kansas City Star
Los Angeles Times
New York Times
Pensacola Daily News
Pensacola Florida Sentinel
Pensacola Journal

Philadelphia Inquirer
Pittsburgh Courier
Pittsburgh Press
Richmond Afro-American
  and Planet
Sheboygan Press
Tuskegee Campus Digest
Wall Street Journal
Washington Post
Wisconsin State Journal

A major collection of individual newspapers useful for a study of Daniel James, Jr., is the Zubkoff Files, Office of Assistant Secretary of Public Affairs, Department of Defense, the Pentagon, Washington, D.C.

Letters

George C. Bales to author, November 26, 1980.
Mabel W. Bates to author, July 14, 1980.
Peter Braestrup to author, October 17, 1980.
General William K. Carr to author, April 27, 1981.
William P. Clements to author, March 20, 1981.
Ray Cron to author, December 1, 1980.
(Lieutenant General) Benjamin O. Davis, Jr., to author, October 16, 1980.
Charles C. Diggs, Jr., to author, October 20, 1980.
Jerry Freidheim to author, October 31, 1980.
Senator Barry Goldwater to author, October 10, 1980.
Bob Hope to author, March 12, 1981.
Colonel Howard C. Johnson to author, January 21, 1980.
Bill Nichols to author, September 24, 1980.
Richard M. Nixon to author, May 18, 1981.
(Brigadier General) Noel F. Parrish to author, January 19, 1981.
H. Ross Perot to author, January 15, 1981.
Robert C. Seamans, Jr., to author, November 19, 1980.
Colonel Thomas C. Wilkinson to author, November 26, 1980.
Bertram W. Wilson to author, October 9, 1980.
Coleman Young to author, November 13, 1980.

Index

Abbott, Cleve, 28
Afro-Union, University of
  Wisconsin, Madison, 129, 130
Air Command and Staff College,
  163
Air Defense Command, 140
Air Force Association, 105, 127
Air Force Equal Opportunity
  Conference, 162
Air Force Times, 158
Air Force Two, 131
Air War College, 162
Alcaniz Street, Pensacola,
  Florida, 15, 16
Alger, Horatio, 5, 159
American Defense Command, 69
American Trucking Association,
  153
Anderson, Charles A. "Chief,"
  31
Anderson, Marian, 137
Andrews Air Force Base, 152
Anzio, Italy, 38
Arizona, University of, 99
Arlington National Cemetery,
  155, 157, 168
Army Regulations 210-10, 42, 47
Ashley, Lieutenant Willie, 40
Associated Press, 125
Atlanta, Georgia, 44

B-1, 147
B-25, 41, 51

BT-13, 36
Baader, Ted "Mother," 64
Baltimore, Maryland, 54
Barnum Day Festival, Bridgeport,
  Connecticut (parade marshal),
  103
Base Rights Agreement (treaty
  with Libya), 109, 113
"Battle Hymn of the Republic,"
  140
Baugh, Captain William J., 74
Bayou Texar, Pensacola, Florida,
  152
Ben Davis's Air Force, 54. See
  also "Black Air Force"
Bentwaters. See Royal Air Force,
  Bentwaters, England
Berry, Danice. See James, Danice
Berry, Colonel Frank (son-in-
  law), 99, 142, 143
Berry grandchildren, 142
"Black Air Force," 48. See also
  Ben Davis's Air Force
Black Flight, 64
Black Leader, 64
Blackman and Robin, 84
Black Panther, 122
Boddie, Colonel James "Tim,"
  Jr., 119
Bolling, Lieutenant George R., 40
Bolo MIG strike, January 2,
  1967, 89, 90, 91, 94
Bowden, J. Earle, 133

Bradley, General Omar N., 169 (n. 3)
Braestrup, Peter, 95
Braniff Airlines, 143
Bridgeport, Connecticut, 103
Briggs, Warren (mayor of Pensacola, Florida), 155
Brooks, Lieutenant Sidney, 40
Brown, Harold (secretary of defense), 152, 153, 156
Brown, Lillie A. *See* James, Lillie A. Brown
Brown, General William Earl, Jr., 119, 154
Bryan, Dr. Herbert L., 171 (n. 34)
Bryant, Paul W. "Bear," 151
Bye, Lieutenant Roger, 78

C-46, 46
C-47, 77
Campbell, Colonel William A., 40, 118
Camp Pendleton, California, 132
Canadian Forces in Ottawa (NORAD), 145
Capen, Dick, 118
Capitol Flying Club, Washington, D.C., 102
Cardozzo, Gerry, 71
Carlton, General P. K., 140
Carmichael, Stokely, 95
Carr, Lieutenant General William K., 146, 147
Carter, Lieutenant Herbert E., 40
Carter, President Jimmy, 147, 152
Carver, George Washington, 22
Cat Bi, Hanoi, North Vietnam, 90
CBS News, 125
Chappie James Appreciation Day, Pensacola, Florida, 103, 166
Cheyenne Mountain, Colorado, 144, 145, 149
Chicago Seven, 128

Chicago Sun, 80
Civilian Aeronautic Administration, 31
Civil rights movement: James's reaction to, 52, 72, 80, 81, 95, 105, 106, 165–67
Clark Air Force Base, Philippine Islands, 56–58, 60, 64, 66
Clements, William P., 138, 140
Clifford, Colonel Thomas E., 119
Coleman, William T. "Bumps," 46
Collins, Dick, 121
Colorado Springs, Colorado, 153, 154
Colorado State University, 103
Columbus, Ohio, 48
Columbus Citizen, 48
Command and Staff College, Maxwell AFB, Alabama, 69, 70
Common Cause, 102
Communists, Filipino, 56. *See also* Huks
Congressional Record, 133
Continental Airlines, 143
Conway, Jim (television program), 103
Cooper, Colonel Charles, 118
Coughlin, William A., 105
Cox, Colonel Hannibal, 118
Crestview, Florida, 102
Cuban missile crisis, 62
Custis, Lemuel R., 37, 40

Dallas, Texas, 130
Da Nang, Vietnam, 90
Daughters of the American Revolution, 137, 140
Davis, General Benjamin O., 35, 40, 53
Davis, Lieutenant General Benjamin O., Jr., 19, 35, 37, 44, 48–51, 53–55, 69, 100, 119, 120, 162
Davis, Rennie, 128

Davis, Lieutenant Richard, 40
Davis, Sammy, Jr., 150, 151, 164
Davis-Monthan Air Force Base,
    Arizona, 80, 82, 88, 120
Dayton, Ohio, 39
De Bow, Charles, 37
De Carlo, Daniel A., 111
Delaware River, 137
Democratic party, Pensacola,
    Florida, 9
Denver Broncos, 150
Detroit, Michigan, 41, 43, 46
Diggs, Representative Charles C.,
    Jr., 72, 100, 101
Distant Early Warning Line, 145
Distinguished Flying Cross, 65
Distinguished Service Medal, 60
Distinguished Unit Citation, 39
Dogpatch base, near Pusan,
    South Korea, 63. See also K-9
    Base
Douglas, Mike (television
    program), 102
Dryden, Lieutenant Charles, 40
Du Bois, W. E. B., 5

Ebony, 131
Edwards, Lieutenant General
    Idwal H., 53, 54
Eglin Air Force Base, Florida,
    51, 98, 99, 100, 107
Eighteenth Fighter Group, 56, 57,
    59
Eighth Tactical Fighter Wing,
    "Wolf Pack," 84, 87, 92, 99,
    121
Eighty-first Tactical Fighter Wing,
    73, 76
Elder, Lee, 154
Elder, Rose, 154
Ellison, Major James A., 39
Emerson Radio Corporation
    Plant, St. Louis, Missouri, 54
Englewood Heights Subdivision,
    Pensacola, Florida, 9

Esso Standard, Libya, 121
Evans, Linda, 128
Evans, Lieutenant Robert, 91
Evans, Rowland, 149
Executive Order 9981, 53

F-4, 77, 82, 85, 87, 90, 91, 92, 93,
    132
F-51, 62, 65, 66
F-80, 62
F-100, 110, 113, 114
F-101A, 75, 78, 82
F-105, 90
Ferocious four, 64
First Artists, 152
Fisk University, 15
Florida, University of, Gainesville,
    127
Florida A & M University, 15,
    19, 29, 71, 99, 143
Florida Jaycees Outstanding
    American Award, 103
Florida Sentinel, 4, 8
Florida State University, 143
Ford, President Gerald R., 46, 60,
    140, 147
Ford, Johnny (mayor of Tuskegee,
    Alabama), 131
Fort Worth, Texas, Chamber of
    Commerce, 102
Fort Walton Beach, Florida, 106
477th Bombardment Group,
    Detroit, Michigan, 41, 44, 45,
    47, 48, 50, 51
437th Squadron, 69
Frazier, Lillie. See James, Lillie
Freedom Foundation Medal, 96,
    99. See also George Washington
    Medal
Freeman Field, Indiana, 45
Freeman Field mutiny, 48
Freidheim, Jerry (assistant
    secretary of defense), 125, 126,
    135, 138, 139
Fuller, Lieutenant Willie H., 40

Gainesville, Florida, 127
Garrison, Colonel Vermont, 87, 117
Geneva Convention, 134
George Washington Medal, Freedom Foundation Contest award, 96. *See also* Freedom Foundation Medal
Gia Lam Base, Hanoi, North Vietnam, 90
Goldwater, Senator Barry, 156
Goodman Field, Kentucky, 45
Greenland Ice Cap, 145
Greensboro, North Carolina, 44

Haiphong Harbor, North Vietnam, 98
Hall, Lieutenant Charles B., 40
Hanoi, Vietnam, 90, 134, 136
Heffernan, Tom, 121
Henkin, Dan (assistant secretary of defense), 118, 124, 134, 138, 139
Ho Chi Minh Trail, Laos, Vietnam, 82, 88
Hoffman, Fred, 125
Hope, Bob, 136
Horatio Alger national award, 137
Houston, Texas, 136
Huks (Filipino communists), 56. *See also* Communists, Filipino
Hunter, Brigadier General Frank O. D., 42, 43, 44, 47

IBM Management Conference, Omaha, Nebraska, 102
Idris, King of Libya, 109, 110, 112
Inchon, South Korea, 64
Inter-Service Club, Madison, Wisconsin, 128
Isis Theater, Pensacola, Florida, 19

Jackson, Jesse, 5, 165
James, Charles (brother), 16, 17, 19
James, Claude "Spud" (son), 59, 82, 99, 142, 143, 155
James, Danice (daughter), 58, 82, 99, 142, 143, 155
James, General Daniel "Chappie," Jr.: birth of, 7, 16; childhood, 16–18; high school years, 18–22; father's death, 22; college years at Tuskegee Institute, 24, 25, 27–40; as football player, 21, 27–29, 50–51, 68; religion of, 26; in Civilian Pilot Training Program at Tuskegee, 31–37; popularity of, 29, 52–53, 59, 78; marriage to Dorothy Watkins, 30; in the Philippines, 56, 66; rescues pilot after crash of a T-33, 60; in Korea, 60–68; leads distinguished mission, 65; and death of Claude "Spud" Taylor, 66; assigned as squadron commander at Royal Air Force Bentwaters, England, 70; rapid rise in rank, 72–73; leadership qualities of, 73–75, 125, 145; in Vietnam, 84, 86–99; attitude toward Vietnam War, 95–98, 102–04, 127–30; after the war, chosen to speak on Vietnam and patriotic subjects, 102; as a celebrated warrior, 102–05; appointment to command Wheelus Air Force Base in Libya, 107, 108, 109–17; assignment to Pentagon, 118; considered by superiors for promotion to general, 118–20; work in public affairs for Defense Department, 124–41; assigned to influence student

opinion, 126; appearances before student audiences, 127–31; as liaison between Defense Department and families of POWs, 135–37; addresses citizen groups, 137–38; receives fourth star, 141; and family life, 141–43; assignment to North American Air Defense, 144–51; hospitalized with heart attack, 150; retirement of, 151, 152–53; in civilian life, 153–54; death of, 154; funeral of, 155, 156 —awards and honors: Barnum Day Festival, Bridgeport, Connecticut (parade marshal), 103; Chappie James Appreciation Day, Pensacola, Florida, 103, 166; Distinguished Flying Cross, 65; Distinguished Service Medal, 60; Distinguished Unit Citation, 39; Florida Jaycees Outstanding American Award, 103; Freedom Foundation Medal, 96, 99; Horatio Alger national award, 137; Legion of Merit Award, 96, 99; Man of the Year Award, Air Force Association, Doolittle Chapter, 148; Man of the Year Award, Kiwanis Club, Pensacola, Florida, 56; Young Man of the Year Award, Massachusetts Chamber of Commerce, 71 —promotions: to second lieutenant, 41; to major, 69; to colonel, 82, 162; to brigadier general, 164; to lieutenant general, 138, 139, 140, 164 —reaction to racial prejudice: in personal life, 34, 106, 130, 133, 137, 151, 163; in the segregated military, 41–55

passim; in the integrated military, 56–58, 71, 72, 74–75, 105, 120, 132, 163 —view of national defense, 127, 128, 147–49, 152

James, Daniel, Sr. (father), 10–12, 15–18, 22, 24, 160

James, Captain Daniel III "Danny" (son), 82, 99, 134, 142, 143, 155

James, Dorothy Watkins (wife), 29, 30, 58, 59, 80, 82, 98, 121, 141–43, 149, 154, 155–56

James, Francis (brother), 17

James, Frank (brother), 17

James, Lillie (sister), 16, 17, 22, 28, 98

James, Lillie A. Brown (mother), 5, 10–18, 23, 24, 34, 139, 159, 160, 161, 163

James, Mason (brother), 17

James, Tony (brother), 17, 22, 98

James, Willie (brother), 17

Jamison, Lieutenant Clarence, 40

Jew in the Box incident, 111

Jim Crow ordinances, 9, 26, 32

Johnson, Lieutenant Howard C. "Scrappy," 64

Johnson, President Lyndon B., 83, 97, 99, 103, 104, 125, 133, 164

Jones, General David C., 145, 146, 149

K-9 Base, Pusan, Korea, 63, 64. See also Dogpatch base

Kennedy, President John F., 72, 78, 125, 148

Kent State University, 76, 124

Kep Base, Hanoi, North Vietnam, 90

Khadafy, Muammar, 109, 110, 111, 112, 114, 115

Khadafy coup, 110

King, Martin Luther, Jr., 4, 81, 105, 106, 131
Kirk, General Bill, 77, 88
Kissinger, Henry, 123
Kiwanis Club, Pensacola, Florida, 133

Lagos, Nigeria, 131
Laird, Melvin (secretary of defense), 116, 118, 119, 124, 128, 133, 134, 138, 139, 156
Lane, Lieutenant Alan, 40
Langley Field, Virginia, 51
Laos, Vietnam, 82, 88, 134
Larson, Swede, 117
Lawrence, Lieutenant Erwin, 40
Lawson, Lieutenant Walter I., 40
LeBailley, General Eugene, 112
Lee, Lieutenant Sterling, 78
Legion of Merit award, 94
Libyan Air Force, 110, 112
Lillie A. James School, Pensacola, Florida, 13–15, 18, 19, 153, 160
Lincoln Memorial, 140
Lockbourne Army Air Field, Ohio, 48, 50–52, 54, 55, 69
Lombardi, Vince, 126
Long, Lieutenant Robert M., 37
Los Angeles Times, 105
Louis, Joe, 16

McAdoo, William, 88
MacArthur, General Douglas, 61, 62, 64, 66, 97
McCaulay, Julie, 107
McDaniel, Vernon, 8, 9, 19, 20
McGee, Colonel Charles E., 118, 119
McLucas, John (secretary of the air force), 139
McNamara, Robert S. (secretary of defense), 83
Macon County, Alabama, 25, 32, 33
Madison, Wisconsin, 128

Maglione, General Ralph "Maggie," 76, 77, 120
Major Bowes Amateur Hour, 22
Manila, Philippine Islands, 56
Man of the Year Award, Air Force Association, Doolittle Chapter, 148
Man of the Year Award, Kiwanis Club, Pensacola, Florida, 56
Marshall, General George C., 47
Marshall, Thurgood, 46
Massachusetts Chamber of Commerce, 71
Maxwell Air Force Base, Alabama, 61, 69, 70
Meade, Major General Henry J., 155
Memphis, Tennessee, 26
Merrill, Gary, 103
MIG, 83, 84, 85, 87, 89, 90, 91, 92, 97
MIG-17, 85
MIG-21, 91, 92, 93
Military Air Lift Command, 140
Mill, John Stuart, 148
Milwaukee, Wisconsin, 153
Mississippi, University of, Medical School, 74
Mitchell, Lieutenant Paul G., 40
Mondale, Vice President Walter, 156
Montgomery, Alabama, 36, 70
Moore, Robert "Red," 27, 30, 34
Morris, Joe, 141
Mustang, 60, 62, 63, 64, 66
Myrtle Beach, South Carolina, 100

NAACP, 30, 46, 47, 81, 157
NATO, 108, 112, 114
NORAD. *See* North American Air Defense; Canadian Forces in Ottawa
Namchonjom, Korea, 65
National Airport, 153, 168
National defense: James's view of,

127, 128, 147–49, 152. *See also*
Vietnam War
National Insurance Agency
Association, Atlantic City, New
Jersey, 102
National League of Families of
American Prisoners and
Missing in Southeast Asia, 134,
135
Naval Air Station, Pensacola,
Florida, 19, 22
Newsweek, 125
New York Times, 95
Nichols, Congressman Bill, 115
Ninety-ninth Pursuit Squadron,
Tuskegee, Alabama, 35, 37
Nishibayashi, Lieutenant
Raymond, 78
Nixon, President Richard M., 46,
97, 117, 123–25, 128, 129, 131,
133, 134, 136
Norman, Lloyd, 125
North Atlantic Air Defense
(NORAD), 139, 144, 164, 165
Norton Air Force Base, San
Bernardino, California, 97
Notre Dame, 28, 73
Novak, Robert, 149

Olds, Brigadier General Robin,
73, 77, 80, 82, 84–89, 91, 94,
97, 99, 102, 117, 121
100 Most Influential Black
Americans, 131
Opera House, Pensacola, Florida,
7
Operation Checkerboard, 43
Operation Happiness, 52
Operation "Rolling Thunder," 83
Orr, Captain Ed, 74, 76, 80
Otis Air Force Base, Cape Cod,
Massachusetts, 69–72, 106

P-40 Warhawk, 36
P-47, 51, 52

Palafox Street, Pensacola,
Florida, 7, 8
Palmer, Joseph (U.S.
ambassador), 112–14
Parrish, Colonel Noel F., 32, 33,
37, 39
Pate, Jerry, 151
Patton, Major Billy, 120
Pensacola, Florida, 4, 7–10, 15–
29 passim, 80, 98, 103, 133,
150, 152, 159, 161, 166
Pensacola, Florida, City Hall, 155
Pensacola Journal, 9
Pentagon, 4, 70, 87, 118, 124,
125, 126, 128, 145, 168, 137–41
People United to Save Humanity
(PUSH), 165
Perot, H. Ross, 135
Peterson Air Force Base, 154
Phuc Yen Base, Hanoi, North
Vietnam, 90, 91
Polesti, 38
POW-MIA wives organization,
124. *See also* National League
of Families of American
Prisoners and Missing in
Southeast Asia
President's Commission on Civil
Rights in the Armed Forces, 72
Price, Colonel Clark, 119, 154
Purnell, Lieutenant Louis R., 40
Pusan, South Korea, 61, 62, 63,
64

Racial prejudice, James's reaction
to: in personal life, 34, 106,
130, 133, 137, 151, 163; in the
segregated military, 41–55
passim; in the integrated
military, 56–58, 71, 72, 74–75,
105, 120, 132, 163
Ragan, Art, 154
Railroad Avenue, Pensacola,
Florida, 10
Raines, Ella, 73

Raspberry, Captain Everett T.,
    92, 93
Rayford, Lieutenant Lee, 40
Red River Valley, 91
Reed, Captain Houghton, 78
Reeves, Cato, 154
Revolutionary Command Council
    (RCC), 113
Richardson, Elliot (secretary of
    defense), 139
Rischer, Lieutenant Colonel Ed,
    77, 78
Risner, Robbie, 117
Rivers, L. Mendel, 100–02, 108
Roberts, Lieutenant George S.,
    40
Roberts, Lieutenant Leon, 40
Rockne, Knute, 28
Rogers, Lieutenant John W., 40
"Rolling Thunder" operation. *See*
    Operation "Rolling Thunder"
Rome, New York, 70
Roosevelt, Eleanor, 47
Roosevelt, President Franklin D.,
    46
Ross, Mac, 37, 39
Route Package 6 (Hanoi-
    Haiphong area), 93
Royal Air Force, Bentwaters,
    England, 70–94 passim, 120,
    121, 141, 150, 154
Ruffles and Flourishes, 152
Rumsfeld, Donald, 156

SA-2, 83
Saigon, Vietnam, 77
St. Joseph's School, Pensacola,
    Florida, 11
St. Louis, Missouri, 54
SAM, 87, 89, 91
San Francisco, California, 77
Schieffer, Bob, 125
Schlesinger, James (secretary of
    defense), 139

Seamans, Robert C., Jr.
    (secretary of the air force), 108,
    139
Selfridge Field, Michigan, 41, 42,
    43, 44, 47
Selma, Alabama, 80
Seoul, South Korea, 61
Sharon, Major Denny, 120
Shaw, Nate, 3, 170 (n. 20)
Shrine of the Immaculate
    Conception, Washington, D.C.,
    155
Sikes, Congressman Robert, 100–
    02, 113, 120
618th Squadron (of the 477th), 44
Sixteenth Air Force, 112
Skinner, B. F., 14
Smith, Lieutenant Graham, 40
Smothers, Curt, 154, 163
Soldiers Field, Chicago, 27
Southern Railroad, 153
"Star Spangled Banner," 138
Stars and Stripes, 95
Steerman biwing airplane, 35–36
Stephen Foster Auditorium,
    University of Pittsburgh, 127
Stimson, Henry (secretary of
    war), 47
Strategic Air Command, 145, 149
Swennes, David, 154
Symington, Stuart (air force
    secretary), 53, 54

T-6, 66
T-33, 60
T-34 (North Korean tanks), 61
Tactical Air Command, 103, 149
Tallahassee, Florida, 29, 71
Taylor, First Lieutenant Claude
    "Spud," 57–59, 64, 66
Taylor, Mrs. Claude "Spud," 59
Thimmesch, Nick, 137, 138
332nd Group (of four black
    squadrons), 37, 39

Thunderbirds, 76
Torch Club, Pensacola, Florida, 133
Tower, Senator John, 156
Townsend, June, 29
Tripoli, Libya, 109, 110, 114
Truman, President Harry S., , 50, 53, 61
Tucson, Arizona, 80
Tucson, Arizona, Country Club, 80
Tuskegee, Alabama, 29, 32, 33, 131, 153
Tuskegee Airmen, 5, 35, 48, 54, 55, 64, 72, 119, 141
Tuskegee Army Air Field, Alabama, 36, 37, 38, 39, 40
Tuskegee Experiment, 31, 32, 33
Tuskegee High School, Tuskegee, Alabama, 29, 132
Tuskegee Institute, 5, 6, 15, 22, 24–37, 42, 44, 72, 100, 105, 119, 159, 162
TWA, 99
Twelfth Fighter-Bomber Squadron, Eighteenth Fighter Group, 57, 58, 60–63, 65, 66
Twenty-fourth Division, 24

Ubon, Thailand, 82–99 passim, 120, 121
United Nations Forces (in Korea), 62, 63, 65, 66
U.S. Air Force Academy, 97, 143, 150, 151, 154
U.S. Air Force Band, 152
U.S. Armed Services Committee, 45, 48
U.S. Department of Defense, 4, 87, 118, 120, 122, 124–26, 133–36, 138, 139
U.S. Department of State, 114, 130
U.S. War Department, 31, 47

University of Akron, 125
University of Louisville, 64
University of Pittsburgh, 127
University of Wisconsin, Madison, 128, 129
Urban League, 81, 131

Vietnam War: James's attitude toward, 95–98, 102–04, 127–30
Volunteer Army, 132

Wade, General H. M., (chief of staff, Supreme Headquarters Allied Powers, Europe), 121
Washington, Booker T., 5, 7, 25, 26, 81
Washington, Mrs. Booker T., 26
Washington, D.C., 5, 46, 61, 71, 99, 101, 109, 128, 135, 145, 153, 155
Washington, George, 137
Washington High School, Pensacola, Florida, 19–21
Washington Post, 97, 98, 122, 156
Watkins, Dorothy. *See* James, Dorothy
Watson, Lieutenant Spann, 40
Wayne, John, 161
Weathermen, 128
West Point, 19, 35, 69, 73, 86
Wheelus Air Force Base, Libya, 76, 107–16, 118, 121, 164
White House, 98, 99, 136, 145, 152, 164
White, Lieutenant Sherman, 40
Wilberforce University, Chicago, 27
Wiley, Lieutenant James, 40
Wilkins, Roy, 81, 157
Wolf Pack. *See* Eighth Tactical Fighter Wing
Womens' Army Corps (WAC), 42
World War I, 35

World War II, 5, 25, 49, 60, 69,
    73, 85–87, 97, 108

Yak (Korean airplane), 62
Young, Coleman, 46
Young, Whitney, 81, 131

Young Man of the Year, 1954,
    award (Massachusetts Chamber
    of Commerce), 71

Zaragoza, Spain, 115
Zuckert, Eugene, 54

James R. McGovern is chairman of the Department of History at the University of West Florida in Pensacola. He received his bachelor of arts degree from Villanova University and his master's and doctorate from the University of Pennsylvania. His publications include *Pensacola 1900–1945: Emergence of a City in the New South* (1976), *Yankee Family* (1978), and *Anatomy of a Lynching: The Killing of Claude Neal* (1982.)